"Wars may be fought with weapons,

but they are won by men.

It is the spirit of the men who follow

and of the man who leads that gains the victory."

—*General George S. Patton*

What Others Are Saying About *Just a Bartender*...

"For years, I sat in church with hundreds of other men listening as Ed Cole taught us that identifying with Christ is the basic principle of Christianity. I'm so pleased today that Ed's son, my friend Paul, is carrying on his ministry. In his new book, *Just a Bartender*, Paul takes this concept of identity and puts a new twist on it using the life of Nehemiah, the cupbearer to the king. Paul explains how when this former slave gets a new identity he changes the world! My prayer is this book will help you find your true identity, so yo*u too can change your world.*"

—*Robert Morris*
Founding Senior Pastor, Gateway Church
Dallas/Fort Worth, TX
Best-selling author, *The Blessed Life, The God I Never Knew, Truly Free,* and *Frequency*

"My wife, Christine, and I are passionate about rescuing trafficked girls. At the end of the day, the problem of trafficking really rests with men. I appreciate Paul Cole's tireless efforts to reach men around the globe with the gospel, and to help men change into men of purpose and grace. Paul's new book, *Just a Bartender*, is exactly what men need to start living up to the identity God has for each of us, and to stop victimizing women and children. I encourage you to get a copy and read it today."

—*Nick Caine*
Cofounder, A21 Network

"Nehemiah was a slave, the cupbearer to the king. As Paul Cole puts it, he was the bartender. After hearing about the ruins of Jerusalem, Nehemiah had more than a change in direction, he had a change in connection. The ancient Hebrew word *shubh* in Nehemiah's great prayer implies taking God from being a great idea to being a great friend, and surrendering to that friend's request. Nehemiah's life illustrates that when men try to live the Christian life without Christ, they are doomed to fail. Christ is the core of our identity, our life, our breath. In *Just a Bartender*, Paul speaks directly to the core of our identity as men, and gives the intended result: that unexpected people change the world."

—*Leonard Sweet*
Bestselling author and professor
Founder and chief contributor to preachthestory.com
Orcas Island, WA

"Years ago I read in Proverbs 18:9, 'Use every endeavor to heal yourself.' Doing exactly that, I won a battle over a life-threatening disease. Often to fulfill our earthly destiny, we have to fight. That's why I appreciate my friend Paul Cole's book about a man's identity. If a man is sick on the inside, he needs to use every endeavor to heal himself. He has to fight. Digesting this book can make you a better husband, a better father, a better man."

—*Casey Treat*
Founding Pastor, Christian Faith Center
Seattle, WA

"Paul Cole provides men help to discover true identity, and end some of the confusion in today's culture. Paul carries on a legacy to speak truth to men, and does so with great strength and perseverance in the face of an increasingly feminized world."

—*Phil Pringle*
Founder, Christian City Churches
Sydney, Australia

"Often it's in the dark times that we get the most clarity—we can see the farthest stars only in the darkest night. When we're clear, focused, and have our identity secure, we can become the men God created us to be. To become a champion, secure in your identity, my brother Paul Cole's book, *Just a Bartender: Unexpected People Change the World*, is a great read for you."
—*Dale C. Bronner*
Founder/Senior pastor, Word of Faith Family Worship Cathedral
Atlanta, GA

"If your desire is to have Christ-loving, family-first, strong men of faith in your church, then I recommend you to Paul Cole. Men are transformed by the strong word Paul delivers. Paul has a huge heart to build strong local churches by building strong men!"

—*Dino Rizzo*
Executive director, Association of Related Churches
Associate pastor, Church of the Highlands
Birmingham, AL

"As much as we don't like to admit it, guys struggle. Paul Cole understands all the issues when it comes to true manhood. He speaks to our issues. He writes about our issues. When Paul speaks, listen. When Paul writes, read. Will you allow me to be candid? What Paul teaches will help you and me to grow up...to be the men that God always envisioned, that we always dreamed of, that our wives always wanted, and our children truly need. Paul wrote it. Get the book. Read it."

—Jim Garlow
Senior pastor, Skyline Church
New York Times bestselling author

"All men are imperfect, but that doesn't mean our identity is tarnished. We are who God says we are from the minute we encounter and accept Christ. That's what happened to Nehemiah, who Paul Cole writes about so brilliantly in his book, *Just a Bartender*. Once a man recognizes his identity, he can start living like the new person God created him to be. Why not start today? Just open the book and read...."

—Leon Fontaine
Senior pastor, Springs Church
CEO, Miracle Channel

"Men don't need another lecture. Men need leadership. In *Just a Bartender*, Paul Cole's leadership shines through. From the biblical character Nehemiah, to a man sitting on an airplane last week, Paul underscores his points using story after story of how ordinary men grew beyond everyday existence to live extraordinary lives that touched the world around them. You'll be enlightened and encouraged through this book."

—Harry Jackson
Senior pastor, Hope Christian Church
Washington, DC

"When I see a book by Paul Cole, I think with appreciation of the hundreds of thousands, and probably millions, of men who have been reached and changed through the ministry of the Christian Men's Network. *Just a Bartender* is about the 'cupbearer to the king,' Nehemiah, and is full of the kind of wisdom you would expect from this ministry, leading men into becoming men of excellence, men with strong spirits, and men with defined purpose. I recommend it."

—Doug Beacham
General Superintendent, International Pentecostal Holiness Church

"There is a frequently used line in African American Church culture that speaks of God as 'a heart fixer and mind regulator.' Paul Cole's book, *Just a Bartender*, presents God as a 'soul fixer'; an eternal, ever-ready Expert who heals the hurts of the souls of men and fixes the heart, while regulating the mind to become the men God intended them to be."

—*Kenneth C. Ulmer*
Senior pastor, Faithful Central Bible Church
Los Angeles, CA

"No one has a greater global ministry in men's ministry that is seeing change by the tens of thousands like Paul Cole—we all have a lot to learn from him."

—*Bob Roberts, Jr.*
Senior pastor, Northwood Church
Keller, TX

"Men today can become loving spouses, better fathers, greater friends, more generous, loving, and compassionate, all by doing one thing—spending time with Jesus. Paul Cole's book draws a man in, leading him to get lost in Christ, and then find himself through Christ. It's an experience I recommend for every man."

—*James Merritt*
Senior pastor, CrossPointe Church
Former president, Southern Baptist Convention
Author, *52 Weeks with Jesus*

"Everyone should have a spiritual mom or a spiritual dad. Ed Cole was a spiritual dad to great leaders, and now Paul Louis Cole is the same. Paul has sat in coffee shops mentoring men literally around the world. In *Just a Bartender*, Paul provides men with the picture of what God expects of us, and who He made us to be. So grab a book and a cup of coffee, and give attention to what Paul has to say."

—*Steve Kelly*
Senior pastor, Wave Church
Virginia Beach, VA

"No man is smart enough to achieve alone God's best results for his life. My friend Paul Cole is reaching out to men to lead them into a closer relationship with God and challenging them to serve their God-given purpose. I commend Paul for his new work, *Just a Bartender*."

—*Tom Lane*
Lead executive senior pastor, Dallas Campus pastor, Gateway Church
Southlake, TX

"Paul Louis Cole is a great friend, a strong leader, a man's man, and when he writes a book, men need to read it! As a leader of men myself, I see *Just a Bartender* tackling the tough problems men face every day, from persevering in negative situations to dealing with an absentee father to tough decision-making. This book is a great tool for men's ministry and an asset for every man."

—*John Bowman*
Men's pastor, Lakewood Church
Houston, TX

"I just finished underlining tons of stuff in this crucial book. I swallowed it in one plane flight and can't wait to give it to many men. It will change them because identity is the crisis of our day. I've been cheered, booed, benched, and cut, but my identity is not my position or performance. Men, we're on an epic journey of purpose. Embracing your identity is essential and this book is dynamite. Nehemiah was a godly stud…and so are you when you embrace God's identity for you."

—*Jeff Kemp*
Former NFL QB
Vice-president, FamilyLife
Author, *Facing the Blitz*

"I was raised by an alcoholic mother and had seven abusive stepfathers pass through my life. The identity crisis my upbringing created lasted through my early manhood. Men need help from biblical answers that really work to become secure in their identity. I commend Paul Cole for writing about a man's identity in a friendly, understandable way that will help a lot of men get set free and get real."

—*Ted Roberts*
Founder, Pure Desire Ministries International
Greshem, OR

"Men often ask me for business advice, and I answer, 'The soul is more important than the goal.' When Jesus renews a man's soul, he's able to achieve his goals. Paul Cole's new book, *Just a Bartender*, is about renewing your soul. I recommend reading it in order to achieve your goals."

—*Peter Lowe*
Business entrepreneur

"Paul Cole points us into character, courage, commitment, and honor in this great new book. In *Just a Bartender*, Paul not only sheds a light on the current challenges men face today, but also shows a pathway on how to find their true identity and how to change the world around them. In times of difficulty or challenge, we need these guiding principles if we as men are to impact the world around us. This book will motivate each of us to make a positive difference, to change the world around us, and to declare, 'I am that man!'"

—*Doug Stringer*
Founder/President, Somebody Cares International
Houston, TX

"I thank God for Paul Cole's honest conversation regarding men who change the world. Paul's blessing to my life and the life of thousands of other men is his gift to encourage undone men that God is not done with. He captures the essence of how God uses the people you least expect to accomplish great things. Get everything he has written into yourself, your sons, your friends, your coworkers, and any other man you meet."

—*Dwayne Pickett, Sr.*
Senior pastor, New Jerusalem Church
Jackson, MS

"Every man is a unique designer original, each endowed with his own identity and with gifts that determine his destiny. When men flounder in their identity, they fail to fulfill God's plan for their life. Most men who abuse women have an identity problem. Solve the identity problem and the man has a chance to honor his wife. Paul Cole's newest book, *Just a Bartender*, takes a man from floundering to flourishing in a new identity. Every man should read it."

—*John H. Binkley, Jr.*
Founder, Generational Group

"Amazing. Paul's unique style of writing weaves the story of Nehemiah with the stories of so many modern-day Nehemiahs and becomes the thread of the fabric in this exceptional book. It's for every person who wants to discover or ignite their purpose, potential, and identity. It's more than a book, it's a pattern that will cause unexpected people to accomplish exceptional things."

—*Rob Carman*
Founder/President, Victory World Missions
Dallas, TX

"Do you know what it takes to be a real man? Do you want to be a real man? For years I did manly things and thought I was all that, but I never knew what being a man really meant. To find your identity as a man, read Paul Cole's new book, *Just a Bartender.* If you want your wife to love you, your kids to respect you, and your future to grow brighter, dig in and read starting right NOW."

—*Ted DiBiase*
"Million Dollar Man"
WWE Wrestler/Hall of Famer
Evangelist, MS

"You're holding in your hand a great read but more than that, you're holding the heart of a great man. Author Paul Louis Cole is one in a million. This offering, *Just a Bartender,* is like spending the weekend with Paul, sitting around a campfire listening to him tell stories. This is the sort of stuff he is made of. I love Paul, who he is, what he stands for, and what he is investing his life in...men. Don't just read this, listen while you read."

—*Lorne Tebbutt*
Founder and senior minister, C3CalgaryWest
Regional Overseer for C3Canada

"Paul Cole is full of fresh perspective and wisdom, and his book, *Just a Bartender,* reflects just that. Men need all the help we can get to think right, in order to act right, live right, and be right. Making a study of this book would be a great exercise for any man. I encourage you to dig right in."

—*Steve Dulin*
Executive Director Gateway Business Leaders
Founding Elder, Gateway Church
Southlake, TX

"Your past doesn't determine your future, but if you don't change your thinking, your past is your future. In Paul Cole's book, *Just a Bartender*, he lays out every man's solution to the identity crisis, helping men think and see ourselves as God does. To live a significant life now and move into an even more significant future, read this book. Because 'unexpected people change the world,' and you just might be the unexpected one we're all waiting for."

—*Joel Brooks*
Senior pastor, Stones Church
Kalamazoo, MI

"Paul Louis Cole is my friend and brother. In Indonesia Christian Men's Network, we have to work with men to understand their identity in Christ before they will change their behavior. And when we do, they begin to love their wives, serve in the community, and help others. *Just a Bartender* will help every man become a better man."

—*Eddy Leo*
Founder, Abbalove and CMN Indonesia

To Lindsay, Niles, Brandon, Meredith, Bryce

I am so intensely proud of you

and so dearly love you.

You are the story I've written

with my life.

JUST A

BAR

UNEXPECTED PEOPLE

TEN

CHANGE THE WORLD

DER

PAULLOUIS**COLE**

W

WHITAKER
HOUSE

R

RESOLUTE BOOKS

JUST A BARTENDER:
Unexpected People Change the World

Christian Men's Network
PO Box 3
Grapevine, Texas 76099

ISBN: 978-1-62911-885-7
eBook ISBN: 978-1-62911-886-4
Printed in the United States of America
© 2017 by Paul Louis Cole

Published by:
Resolute Books™
Whitaker House
1030 Hunt Valley Circle
New Kensington, PA 15068
www.whitakerhouse.com

Library of Congress Cataloging-in-Publication Data
LC record available at https://lccn.loc.gov/2017009021

3 4 5 6 7 8 9 10 11 12 **LU** 24 23 22 21 20 19 18

CONTENTS

FOREWORD

Whatever has defined you to this point, *Just a Bartender* will help you discover and release the dream, the passion that lies within your inner self, that defines *who* you really are.

Using the life of Nehemiah, the "cupbearer" from Scripture, Paul Louis Cole has created a great analogy for any man—a bartender! **Nehemiah was a bartender and a slave, but rose to prominence as a leader and saved his nation. He's proof that "unexpected people change the world."**

Nehemiah was more than just a slave, and you are more than just a..._____(*fill in your blank*).

Many of us get caught up in what we see around us. We have a goal to reach certain heights—to buy a new house, or get a bonus, or put our kid in a certain school, or receive a promotion, or start a new relationship, or win an NBA Championship. While any of these things may be good—and winning championships feels great!—they still don't satisfy the inner desire and dream of a heart that has not resolved the question: *am I living to the full capacity of my life or is there more?*

Getting caught up in "Do, do, do; conquer, conquer, conquer; action, action, action; results, results, results" can pacify us but bury the real, true inner issues of our lives. Temporary satisfactions, rewards, trophies, merits, and championships are great things in their own right but will not fill you to your full capacity. And, not achieving them can be crushing.

Just a Bartender will help you. I'd like to give some copies to people I know who don't feel like they're living out their destiny. For a guy fresh out of the prison system—please understand that a cell may be where you *were*, but that doesn't mean it's who you *are*. For people who are trying to get back on track—please understand that your future is determined by *not* letting others define you.

When your thoughts change, so will your future change. You do have hope, and you have more than just an ordinary purpose, because "unexpected people change the world."

—*A.C. Green*
NBA Ironman
Los Angeles

1
STORY

Josh says he knows almost every customer that comes into his bar. He knows their dreams and disappointments, their defeats and desires. He says, "Everyone has a story. And I think I've heard most of them. Too often, in huge detail."

I ask, "So, how many people know *your* story?" Behind us, a barista turns up the steam on a latte as early morning customers hurry in and out. I'm listening. Josh is hesitant. At least he's here.

"Nobody cares about my story," he says. "They just care about whether the beer is cold."

A veteran of intense military battles, Josh has a dramatic story, but no one is listening. He's just a bartender. Just there to provide a good buzz and a listening ear.

Bartenders and hair stylists...they know everyone's story, but not many know theirs. They listen. Customers talk. Customers know what they do, but not who they are.

There's another man people didn't notice much. Nehemiah was the bartender for a king—and he was a slave. Slaves don't have notable stories—particularly not a story a king would want to hear. So, while the king talked, Nehemiah the bartender listened. And, like my friend Josh, Nehemiah saw and heard some very private matters, especially as the king or his guests drank and feasted. He knew their stories…but they didn't know his.

How many people know who *you* really are? Who knows your story?

For most of us men, we are identified by what we do with our hands…manager, fireman, sales executive, forklift driver, physical therapist, flooring installer, school principal, carpenter.

One of the first things we ask when meeting another man is, "What do you do?" Then we slot that man. Our minds work better when he's slotted. We have a point of reference.

But is what you do who you really are?

Culture defines a man by what he does with his hands. God defines a man by who he is in his heart.

It was around 450 BC when Nehemiah served King Artaxerxes, ruler of the Persian Empire and much of the known world. Nehemiah's official title was "Cupbearer to the King." His job was a trustworthy position. It involved mixing the king his favorite drinks, keeping the king's liquids safe, holding his confidences, and taking a few risks— like ensuring the drinks had no poison by tasting them first himself.

Nehemiah was a bartender and a slave, a man who had earned the trust of his master, and perhaps the respect of his peers. That was his job and his position in life. But it was not his identity.

One afternoon his brother came with bad news. The city of Jerusalem was destroyed and in ruins. Jerusalem, the royal city of David. Jerusalem, the very center of Nehemiah's culture, his religion, the embodiment of his people's identity. In Nehemiah's quiet thoughts, Jerusalem contained all his hopes and dreams. It was a city the Hebrew slaves prayed for—for *"the peace of Jerusalem."*[1] The city they all hoped to see one day.

Overrun by wars and marauding armies, the city of Jerusalem had been in ruins for almost one hundred years. But as far as Nehemiah knew, people had gone there to rebuild it. To Nehemiah, busy in the palace, Jerusalem seemed a world away. In his mind, work on the historic city was underway by other people entrusted to the task and expected to do their job. But now his brother tells him Jerusalem is a huge mess. The men there live in constant fear, too oppressed and hopeless to risk rebuilding. The city itself has been unoccupied for so long, the ruins so badly decomposed, that the destruction now appears permanent.

Nehemiah's heart is devastated. The entire city wiped out? The capital of his people, the pride of the nation, their religious identity—*destroyed? Gone?*

In the privacy of his basement quarters, the deep pain and disappointment double him over. He's a slave in a foreign country. Now, his dreams of one day seeing Jerusalem seem like just a fantasy. Hope is smashed to ruins.

Despair overwhelms him. Can't sleep, can't eat—so he starts fasting. He starts praying. First for hours, then for days, going through work then rushing back to his room and dropping to his knees. Alone. With God. Searching God's heart, and his own. In those solitary, desperate hours, there seems to be no hope. Then, as the intimacy of prayer unclouds Nehemiah's broken spirit, he asks himself, *Is there a path? Who do I know that could get this done? It's impossible. How could I do anything? Could I do something? What would that look like? I know I wasn't born to be just a slave....*

It's a variation of one of the most important questions we must ask ourselves as men:

Is the level of life I am now living at the full capacity of my life?

Are we living at our maximum, or is there another level? Are we at full capacity, or is there more? *IS THIS IT?*

And perhaps:

What do I do to get out of here? Is there a path?

Nehemiah has a great job, but he's still a slave. Like many men, he's subject to the circumstances and coincidences and stuff that just happens. Also like many men, he's reached heights of outward merit or reward, but the truest desires and dreams of his heart go unresolved.

No matter our position or awards or acknowledgments, no matter whether we're standing in the shadows of a world that has roared past us, no matter if we're somehow being carried along in the middle of a crowd feeling like the Eagles song, "Your prison is walking through this world all alone"[2]: we may not be lonely, but we're alone.

What we whisper to ourselves when life gets us honest is often…

Is this my reality? Am I locked into this path of being a barista/ an insurance salesman/a corporate executive/trapped by debt or a mortgage when I have other things inside that move me deeply, that I know I'm capable of? Will I never go after what really makes me come alive? Can I even express it? I'm not sure….

Most of us have something larger inside us—it's just locked up. The revelations found in the story of Nehemiah can put our lives on a new path. Nehemiah was a slave, but he was a slave who had a dream. And he committed to his dream.

We become the size of the dreams we are courageous enough to pursue.

Or we shrink to the size fear allows us to become…which is always smaller than what we were designed by God to be.

Everywhere Nehemiah turned, he faced an enemy. The enemy of self-doubt, the enemy of slavery, the enemy of chaos, disappointment, distraction. All that, plus the original enemy behind it all—the one who kicks your butt almost every week. Jesus called out this enemy—he is Satan. He's the enemy who tried to kill Jesus and is trying to kill you, too. There are many ways to die—the death of a career, a dream, a relationship.

That enemy of all men wants to rip out your heart and cause you to quit. This enemy is after your *identity*. What *is* your basic identity? This: You were made in the image of God, and you were born for a purpose. You have ideas, dreams, and thoughts about your life. You are uniquely you.

Your identity is the story you tell yourself about yourself.

Too often, the story men tell themselves is based on the words they heard from someone else. Too often, it's the negative words that stick. But the more you lean into God, the clearer your purpose becomes, the more positive your personal narrative, and the greater your potential for success.

A great example of the power of identity is the proportionally large number of Jewish people who have excelled in Nobel Prizes, literature, finance, science, media, and many more stunning achievements. It turns on one small habit they have practiced for centuries. As children, they gather around their father, who reads stories of their Jewish heritage, not as ancient history, but as the story of *who we are*. By the time a young man or woman is in their teens, they have a powerful grasp of *identity*. That identity sharpens their focus, empowers their decision making, and enlarges their tenacity.

But, *if the enemy can steal your identity—he can control your heart.* And it's from your heart that the story of your life unfolds.

The enemy wanted to keep Nehemiah behind a bar as a slave, to stop his story from breaking loose. It's no different for you. The enemy wants to keep you in slavery—a slave to negative emotions, discouraged words, and corrupted instincts. But any man can break free. The amazing thing is, when you break free, the people around you will get their chance to be free, too.

Two men in the first century illustrate this. Paul and Silas were a couple of young, hardworking followers of Jesus. Because they talked about their faith, magistrates in a Roman city ordered them to be beaten and thrown into the local dungeon—not a great place to be.

At midnight, deep in the darkness of the dank squalid hole carved out of the side of a hill, Paul and Silas start singing. They sing of their faith. Songs of praise and joy. Jesus is Lord. God is my shepherd. On and on. The other men in prison listen (as if they had a choice). As they sing, a sudden earthquake shakes the city. The dungeon doors fly open. Paul and Silas's chains drop off them...*and every other prisoner's chains drop off, too.* When Paul and Silas have their breakout moment—it becomes a breakout moment for everyone around them.

There are people in your life who are just waiting for you to break free, because when you get set free, they'll be set free. There are people in your world who will not get their breakthrough until you grab your breakthrough. In that prison, it may have seemed like just some guys singing, but their words shook the heavens.

Keep vigilant watch over your heart;
that's where life starts.[3]

Josh sits, quiet. Pensive. Thinking. Gripping a double latte. He's made some bad mistakes, and is now just tending bar and hanging out—waiting for something, but he doesn't know what. So I ask him the question, "Is the level of life you are now living at the full capacity of your life?"

"No!" he says, as if I didn't have to ask. He knows he has dreams and thoughts, but he is treated as if he has none, and it messes with his identity. We pause, then I say, "Josh, are you willing to start reframing the story you tell yourself about yourself?"

"Yes," is his quiet answer.

We prayed and Josh started. The last time I saw Josh, he had found it was more fulfilling to sell insurance to people who needed it than booze to people who didn't. He had a good girlfriend, was about to get engaged. None of it was easy. It took time. But now he's writing the story he always wanted to live.

Josh *started.*

2
START

The opposite of fear is...*start*.

Lions can actually paralyze animals they're hunting by the massive infrasonic fierceness of their roar. Fear comes like a roaring lion seeking to paralyze you, keeping you from living the story you know you should live. Fear roars at you every day. Fear doesn't like you. Fear wants you to fail—because then fear wins.

The only way you can succeed is to start. The only sure way *not* to succeed is *not* to start. Everything God has ever done has been successful. In fact, God has never had an unsuccessful thought.

Success is what God *does*.

And God had the prophet Jeremiah write down exactly what God thinks about you: "I *know* what I'm thinking about you. It's surely not about your destruction—in fact, it's about a successful future and a life full of hope!"[1]

When we accept the definitions of a failed culture, we accept its failure. The true definition of success is not what the world says. Success means to fully satisfy your personal design. Grab that. Read it again. Here goes:

Success is to fully satisfy your personal design.

Success is to become everything God designed you to be—what you deeply desire to be. Success isn't about position or applause—it's about the deep-felt satisfaction of knowing you've lived out your life as strong as you could. If you're a forklift driver, strive to be the best. If you're selling insurance, aspire to be the top salesman in your district. If you're teaching, win the kids' hearts.

Paul, who wrote much of the New Testament, paraphrased Solomon the king:

> *"Whatever you do,*
> *work at it with all your heart."*[2]

Some translations say, *"...work from the soul"*[3] And others say, *"...do it heartily."*[4]

That. Is. Success. Not that you succeeded or failed in the eyes of the world—but that, at end of the day, you did everything with absolute full intensity. You did not hold back one bit of sweat, effort, or guts. You went after success from the depths of your heart.

When you have success, it may never be seen. It's yours and God's. When you have success, it's *your* success. The author Steven Pressfield said he got great satisfaction when he reached the end of his first novel and wrote the words "The End." But that novel never sold. He never got a penny for it. No one ever read it. Yet the *success* of finishing made him realize he could achieve his dream. So he wrote another novel. And another. And became a successful author.

God has a unique purpose for the life of every person. I was told as a young man that God loves me and has a wonderful plan for my life. What kept me up nights was the question, *What if I can't find the plan?*

But to paraphrase my friend Len Sweet, God loves you and has a *purpose* for your life—and an unstoppable *plan* for the world. Your *purpose* is your outline. You didn't miss the *plan*. So, go write the story. Now. Start.

Ed is a close friend whose life trajectory was like so many men's, yet whose outcome was astonishingly different. Ed was the product of a religious tradition that was based on obeying rules and regulations. Ed laughs, "We had rules even God couldn't obey." By the time he hit his adult years, he had left the church. He decided he would find a way to make it on his own.

Then he met Barbara. Barbara is full of life...and full of fun. I know, because she is one of my wife's dearest friends. The wedding day came and it was *on*. Barbara had children when she married Ed, and together they had more. Everyone was looking to Ed to provide for them. He had a job in a restaurant corporation, then another job...and then years later the jobs were gone.

Ed realized he was at the end as he played a daily dance with financial ruin. He had very little relationship with his children. He and Barbara didn't agree on anything—they were both *done*. Work, kids, wife, all against him. Ed says, "If I'd owned a dog, the dog would've bitten me." Just as he was about to say "forget it" and walk away, a neighbor invited him to a men's meeting.

At that point, Ed hadn't been able to find another corporate position so he had started his own small business driving a lumber truck from Redding, California, to Los Angeles. Six days a week he trekked his International diesel up and down the state. But this Saturday, he made time to go to the men's event.

He walked into the meeting and was shocked to see hundreds of men there. The speaker was my dad, Edwin Louis Cole. Dad said at that meeting, "Most men have been trained to hear sermons, not study the Word of God."

Truck driver Ed realized that, as a rule, he never cracked open a Bible. He also heard that truth is like soap, it doesn't work unless it's applied.

At the end of the meeting, he bought one each of the books and recordings available. That night, Ed watched his family head to bed, then grabbed his Bible and lay on the living room floor, face down.

He said, "God, I don't know how to study the Bible. I don't know how to live according to Your Word. But I'm opening it now." He opened the Bible in front of him and continued, "I'm asking You to teach me. And if this doesn't work out, then…it's *Your* fault."

Over the next four years, Ed listened to cassette tapes on a tape player above his head in the cab of that diesel truck. He studied the Word of God every night in dank motels on the edge of the highway and kept his Bible handy to read during the hours it took guys to load and unload his truck. He stayed at it. Barbara began to notice a difference. Slowly, things began to change.

Ed began to reframe his story and regain his dreams. He and Barbara returned to the restaurant business—but this time as owners. They started small with the whole family involved. Today, it's been twenty years and they have highly successful Biscuits Café restaurants across the western US. Ed knows that getting the Word into his heart, repenting to God and his wife, reading the Bible, listening to the teaching, and letting God renew his mind changed everything.

THE BEST WAY TO START IS TO *START*.

The Ed that lay on the floor that night and prayed his simple prayer is not the same Ed I know today. Ed wasn't perfect after that prayer. The prayer was the *start*. The prayer was pushing *play*. The prayer was hitting *enter*. The prayer was turning the *ignition*.

The difference between Ed and so many others is that he *started*. And once he started, he didn't quit. He got focused, saw purpose, and it was addictive. He read his Bible, did what it said, prayed more, and now he's fulfilling his purpose, and his family is living a highly successful, deeply satisfying life.

I've been privileged to meet some high-net-worth individuals, rock stars of business, media and, well, rock music. And of all the training and motivating stories I've ever heard, the greatest advice is this: the best way to start is to *start*.

It sounds simplistic—but it has always been a biblical truth. **Simple obedience solves complex issues.** God loves men who start. God is a champion of small beginnings. It doesn't mean that you start a business without a plan. But, if you want to launch something new, then at the very least *start* the planning and the research.

God loves stuff that starts.
So He created seeds.

Years ago a wonderful friend motivated dozens of young men to follow their dreams into their destinies. I thought Dr. Ed Neteland must have a special formula, a depth of counsel that was otherworldly. One day I asked him, "Ed, how does that happen? How do you advise them?"

He said he would simply sit the young man down in his boardroom with a piece of paper and a pen—then ask two things:

What would you do if money were not an issue?
What would you attempt if you knew you would not fail?

"Then," he said, "I tell them to come back to me when they have their answers written down. That starts the process of reframing their goals and dreams."

Our issue is that the start looks small. **The most difficult discipline in the life of a leader is to be faithful…in the small things.**

Start!

Now.

Right now!

3

DIG

As he heard the news that Jerusalem was in ruins, Nehemiah's heart was battered, his spirit devastated, his mind overwhelmed and perplexed. *Jerusalem destroyed? How could this happen? It's so wrong! What have those locals been doing? What can I do? What can anyone do?*

To start, Nehemiah did something most men overlook. He put off the increasingly negative thoughts...and he prayed. It wasn't a prayer of resignation, or defeat, or despair, or denial. Nehemiah prayed *life* into the deadening reality of the situation. He prayed into the aliveness of his God. He prayed in faith. Faith trusts God no matter what the conditions look like.

Nehemiah is kneeling in a slave's apartment—fasting from food, praying, and praying some more. He would appear to be just a solitary slave sending plaintive appeals into thin air, yet his prayers are reframing his heart. And then, his prayers electrify all of human history.

Every day, we are bombarded with hundreds of thousands of messages—the equivalent of 174 newspapers every day. We hear hundreds of opinions and negative news reports. We get blasted by the 29,500,000 trillion (that means you add 12 more zeroes) pieces of information in the world. And it keeps compounding. That's a lot of traffic across our minds and spirits...and it never seems to quiet down.

What was Nehemiah doing? He was digging in. Getting focused. **Focus is the discipline of extracting yourself from the unnecessary.** Prayer is the most powerful tool we have available to focus our hearts.

Prayer strips away the inconsequential.

Why did Jesus invest so much of His time in prayer? Why couldn't He, God Incarnate, just say, "I've got this"?

Like you and me, everywhere Jesus turned, someone wanted Him to do something: "Heal me." "Come this way." "Pay attention to me." "Fix this." "Help me." "Teach me." Jesus faced nonstop requests to come to someone's town, heal their son, fix their synagogue, answer their questions, attend a party, provide fish and bread. Jesus' life was a never-ending stream of questions, accusations, requests, and chaos. Prayer centered the humanity of Jesus. It brought clarity into His humanness.

Clarity always defeats chaos.

Jerusalem was a place Nehemiah had never seen, yet it was at the center of his family heritage. He didn't have to see the city to know his identity was tied to it. He had been taught that since his earliest days. Though he was a slave, he dreamed of one day actually walking into the holy city of Jerusalem. The parting greeting he and all Jews gave each other, whether slave or free, was always, "Next year, in Jerusalem."

MATURITY DOESN'T COME WITH AGE, IT COMES WITH THE ACCEPTANCE OF RESPONSIBILITY.
—EDWIN LOUIS COLE

Nehemiah faced a crushing and overwhelming negative report. It was so devastating, he cried out in anguish and pain, and then prayed. It wasn't just a short, "Hey God, You there?" Or, "Bless the food." Or, "Now I lay me down to sleep." His prayer went on for days. Then, after all the fasting, all the praying, all the gut-wrenching tears, we hear his final prayer—maybe a condensed version—in the very first section of his memoir, right after the bad news.

1. REPENTANCE!

Nehemiah *starts* with this:

> O LORD, God of heaven, the great and awesome God who keeps his covenant of unfailing love with those who love him and obey his commands, listen to my prayer! Look down and see me praying night and day for your people Israel. I confess that we have sinned against you. Yes, even my own family and I have sinned! We have sinned terribly by not obeying the commands, decrees, and regulations that you gave us through your servant Moses.[1]

This is a huge principle for success. Nehemiah opens by acknowledging that his people, his nation, had messed up. Then he embraces the issues and admits that he and his family also messed up. He's not pointing fingers or making accusations. He takes personal responsibility and apologizes. This is the strength of a mature man.

In these statements we see the first glimpse of the character of Nehemiah—and discover his strength as a real man. My father said it this way: Maturity doesn't come with age, it comes with the acceptance of responsibility.

After admitting liability, Nehemiah asks God to forgive him and his nation. He doesn't play around with the issues. He faces reality. This is a man with some backbone, character that doesn't look for excuses or blame someone else. This is true manhood.

"It's clear—we have messed up. I own it, and now I repent."

Repentance is always the first step toward renewal. From repentance comes reconciliation, then restoration, then renewal. The prayer of repentance brings reconciliation with God who restores our original design and imputes renewal into our hearts. It is the path to reframing our story—the renewal of our thinking.

No repentance—no renewal.

2. THE WORD!

Nehemiah's intense prayer continues:

> *Remember the instruction you gave your servant Moses, saying, "If you are unfaithful, I will scatter you among the nations, but if you return to me and obey my commands, then even if your exiled people are at the farthest horizon, I will gather them from there and bring them to the place I have chosen as a dwelling for my Name."[2]*

Nehemiah does what great leaders since David have learned to do—pray the Word of God. What touches, changes, and transforms our hearts is not just a great talk or awesome music. What brings the greatest change to any person is the Word of God. The Word can do more in a man's heart than the greatest of sermons.

The Bible is not just a handbook for daily living, a guide to wisdom, or a series of "How to Live" essays. The Bible is the highest manifestation of God Himself on the face of the earth. Everything flows from God's presence.

WHEN YOUR THOUGHTS CHANGE, YOUR FUTURE CHANGES.

Nehemiah quotes God's Word. Not because God might forget—but to say out loud what God has promised, what he needs to hear to remind himself of God's goodness. Hearing the Word lifts Nehemiah's heart and brings him to a place of boldness. The Word always enlarges a man's heart; being "Wordless" always shrinks it.

The Word is the transformative substance that changes the path of your thinking. When your thoughts change, your future changes.

3. ASK!

Next, Nehemiah prays this:

> *"They are your servants and your people, whom you redeemed by your great strength and your mighty hand. Lord, let your ear be attentive to the prayer of this your servant and to the prayer of your servants who delight in revering your name. Give your servant success today by granting him favor in the presence of this man."*[3]

The lesson is—*approach boldly.*

When I was a child, I didn't think about the ramifications of asking my dad for a bicycle or a baseball bat. I just asked. It may have been bold but I didn't know that. It was what I wanted—and he was my dad. It came naturally, out of relationship.

Boldness comes from intimacy. Nehemiah's boldness was not the insolence of a braggart or the hubris of a fool. It was the asking that comes from closeness. Nehemiah already knew where God was leaning because it was in His Word. So, he just put himself and his prayer into alignment with the Word of God.

The prayer of a mature man. A man who is willing to pay the price, take the pain, work the strategy, to see his dreams come to pass.

As he closed his prayer, Nehemiah made two specific requests:

Success and Favor

Too often, our little myopic, near-sighted prayers center on "whatever you will, God." But Jesus told us to pray bold prayers. To pray as though something depends on it. It does.

James, the half-brother of Jesus, wrote, "You don't have what you really desire, because you don't ask for it."[4] We don't have to act holy so God can see how good we are—hoping maybe then He'll give us something. He's not impressed. He's not manipulated. He's above all that.

Too often we don't ask for success because it sounds arrogant or, at the least, not very humble. At the churches I attended as a child, we often looked at highly successful people with some apprehension, as if perhaps they had compromised to get there. That was based on a failed and narrow viewpoint that still pollutes men's dreams today.

What you allow to define you will determine your destiny. Too often we accept the empty definitions of men's philosophies because they appear to be holy. Or we slide to the other side and arrogantly demand "rights," using the definitions of a self-serving, pagan culture. Both are wrong.

Nehemiah prayed for *favor*. Favor is when God leans into your dreams. Favor is deep approval, being given preference over others. Favor is to be put in high regard because of relationship, not performance.

Paul wrote, "God has freely given to us every spiritual blessing.... *He has put favor on us.*"[5] Another translation reads that He has *"accepted"* us.[6] That's favor—to be accepted by God no matter where we've been, what we've done, what has happened to us—*and to get every blessing* because of it. Paul is saying to you and to me: from our rotten mess, God writes a fresh story.

Moses was a Jewish baby slated for death, but his mom worked out a plan that caused the Pharoah's daughter to adopt him. Then the Pharoah—the very one who put out a death warrant for all Jewish boys—accepted this Jewish boy into the palace. Moses was accepted, now he had even more—he was a son. Favor!

Mary, the mother of Jesus, was greeted by the angels with the words, "The Lord is with you, you are blessed and highly favored."[7] Wow, highly favored...because the Lord is with you. Favor!

Look at these men in the Bible. They had *favor*!

+ God told **Gideon**, "*The* LORD *is with you.*"[8]

+ **Joseph** had the favor of his father.[9]

+ God said to **Moses and Abraham**, "*I will be with you.*"[10]

+ Jesus told the **disciples**, "*I'll be with you as you do this, day after day after day, right up to the end of the age.*"[11]

They had favor, but these men also had to dig in and fight. The first level of warfare is prayer. Prayer activates the armies of heaven.

Nehemiah's prayer was not that of just a slave. It was the prayer of a man who trusted God. It cut through the peripheral, gave his life focus, clarified his purpose, and put into motion things that would alter world history. His prayer engaged and embraced his identity.

Prayer is the most important tool to give your life the story you desire. There is one important move to make right now...start digging. It's called *prayer*.

You just have to *ask*.

4

TENACITY

Nick Vujicic was born with a rare disorder—he has no arms and no legs. For many men, this would be the end. No dreams, no future. But Nick is a man of tenacious faith. Despite suffering from bullying, and struggling mentally and physically, he didn't give up.

Today, Nick is a father and husband, and a well-known motivational speaker and author. He writes about life, love, and self-acceptance. He writes about family, productivity, and work. He writes about the power of faith and of standing strong.

Nick says, "Keep moving ahead because action creates momentum, which in turn creates unanticipated opportunities."[1] Nick had to build his life day by day, layer upon layer, defeat and success, joy and pain, brick upon brick—until he achieved his dreams. There is no easy way.

———

Nehemiah continued going to work every day. But over time, the king noticed a deep shift in his mood. Finally, the powerful Artaxerxes asked Nehemiah what was distracting him, making him so preoccupied. He asked the bartender for his story. At that moment, fear gripped Nehemiah. He faced the decision that men everywhere face.

Would he plunge forward and endure the pain? Would he tell the king and risk being imprisoned, scorned, flogged, demoted? Would he push through temporary discomfort in order to achieve the dream? We are all risk averse—it's in our nature—and it was in Nehemiah's.

Nehemiah is a Persian slave. He's a nobody. He's at huge risk if he acts. Nehemiah can speak up, or he can retreat inside himself and rationalize away the need for courage. Rationalizing is so easy:

"I've prayed, and God can just make this happen without me having to say anything."

"The king wouldn't care about a conquered people far away."

"I'm lucky enough to have this good job and the king's favor. I don't want to risk it."

Nehemiah could step back and watch what happened to his beloved city, his homeland, and all his friends and relatives. Or he could step up and stand strong as he opened his mouth to tell the king what was wrong.

President Teddy Roosevelt said it this way: "Far better it is to dare mighty things, to win glorious triumphs, even though checkered by failure, than to take rank with those poor spirits who neither enjoy much nor suffer much, because they live in the gray twilight that knows not victory nor defeat."[2]

Faith in God is the foundation for a successful life. Faith gives power to our dreams. Then we have to go to work. James wrote, *"Faith without works is dead."*[3]

The universe is not arrayed to work in your favor. The world will always conspire with your enemy, the devil, to destroy you. *Victory is always on the other side of the fight.* Faith gets up and works. And endurance never lets go.

If you're moving forward, obstacles will appear. If you want a life without obstacles or without a fight...stand silently in the shadows... but they'll still find you. If you're never criticized, your dreams are too small.

A smack in the face will stop most men, but it comes with pursuing the dream. My friend Big Tommy Sirotnak used to say, "If you're on a road that has no obstacles, you're on the wrong road!" Tenacity will power a man through the hits and criticisms.

FAITH GETS UP AND WORKS. AND ENDURANCE NEVER LETS GO.

Not knowing exactly what to do, Nehemiah did what he knew to do. He got up and went to work every day. Day after day, he worked. Night after night he prayed. Most men won't pay the price for their dreams. Nehemiah wasn't most men—he tenaciously held on.

Paul wrote, "What you really want you don't get, because you lack endurance."[4]

Tenacity, boldness, endurance, sweat—nothing happens without that.

You can have visions and dreams, but without the guts of endurance to sustain you, it will never happen. I've had coffee shop meetings with many young men who want to start something—a business, a church, a music venture, an educational program. When I talk about the launch that will include 7-day workweeks and 14-hour days, their enthusiasm diminishes.

Some men are not praying for *miracles*, they're hoping for *magic*. God is a miracle-worker, not a magician. You do your part, He does His. Nothing great happens without work. Nothing great happens without a tenacious spirit. Nothing great happens without the price of pain attached. And the price of pain may come often as we trust God in the midst of our human fears, doubts, and disappointments.

Think deeply. Pray hard. Act aggressively. Never quit.

General George S. Patton said, "A good plan violently executed now is better than a perfect plan executed next week."[5]

I get to Main Street Cafe early and stir a sprinkling of sugar into a cup of Italian brew. Marcos comes and soon we are in the thick of his business meltdown. Nothing is going right. He has known success, built businesses before, but this time it's all different. Everything he owns is at risk. One more setback and thirty years of sweat and effort will be gone...not to mention his house, the cars, the furniture, maybe everything. It's a precarious edge.

We talk for a while, then step outside and sit in his car to pray. Paul and Silas's earthquake doesn't show up—no lightning, just a moment of "Nehemiah style" prayer together concerning a massive obstacle. After we have joined our hearts in prayer, I ask him, "What next?"

He says, "I'm headed to the office to do what I know to do. I'm expecting God to show up...somehow. I'm at peace. Thanks."

He leaves, and the next day he texts. After we prayed, things got worse. The next day—worse again. The following week, a mild improvement. At least there's no bad news. Meeting together over the next few months, it seems at every turn there's a little more light, a few small victories. Over months, then over years, the small victories turn into big wins. The last time I saw Marcos, his company was larger than he ever imagined it could be.

What did he do? He didn't let go, he was tenacious. He listened to trusted counselors. He prayed with his wife. He admitted his need and prayed with close friends. Marcos trusted God with everything, then he went to work. In other words, he did what a man does.

> **"Nothing in the world can take the place of persistence. Talent will not; nothing is more common than unsuccessful men with great talent. Genius will not; unrewarded genius is almost a proverb. Education will not; the world is full of educated derelicts. Persistence, determination alone are omnipotent."**
> —*Calvin Coolidge*[6]

It's early and already hot. August in Texas. I'm at the Starbucks on Highway 26 and Glade Road. Brent rocks up as I'm settling down to a perfect triple-shot tall vanilla latte. He's meeting me for "coffee," but walks in carrying a huge Big Gulp cup dripping with condensa-

IF YOU'RE NEVER CRITICIZED, YOUR DREAMS ARE TOO SMALL.

tion. He explains he never got the coffee habit because of his athletic training. But he admits he did acquire a taste for certain other beverages.

An outstanding high school athlete and scholar, Brent won a scholarship to a prestigious university. After a year, his drinking and out-of-control lifestyle led the school to vacate his spot. He came home devastated, embarrassed. He knocked around and finally found work doing security at a bar. As he journeyed back into his faith, he stopped drinking, got sober, and started a fence-building business by day while working at the bar by night. Then he met a beautiful young lady named Danielle.

Today, we talk about the youth football teams he's enjoyed coaching this summer. Local high school coaches know him and rumor has it that some are talking about the results he's getting with the young athletes. Football is his passion, and coaching young men is the most satisfying thing he's ever done.

I tell Brent about the time my friend Steve and I coached our sons on a youth baseball team. We had fun. It was a great year. As I recall it I think, *One of the best things a young man could have in his life is a coach like Brent—a great athlete who has made mistakes but has come through the other side as a real man.*

Brent is unhappy. Frustrated. "Things are finally breaking your way," I tell him. "What makes you so unhappy about that?" I already know the answer: he's not living at the full capacity of his life. But he needs to articulate it.

"Because I want to marry Danielle, but first I need a good job. To get a job coaching, I need a state certificate. Because I messed up, I still need another twenty-eight units of college for my degree before I can even take the certification test."

"How long will it take?"

"Well, I'm taking three units this semester and three next semester…so, really, in about five or six years, I'll have it."

I can see how this sounds like forever to a vibrant twenty-three-year-old. It sounded like a long time to me, too.

I tell him about an old friend named Dave. Years ago, a group of friends were at our house in the San Francisco East Bay area where Judi and I lived when we were first married. We were talking about dreams and deep desires when the subject came up that Dave wanted to be a doctor. Everyone sitting in the living room begins encouraging him to do it. But Dave laments, "Oh man, if I go back to school to become a doctor, it's going to take ten more years. I'll be thirty-six by the time I get out!"

At that point our friend Steve shouts from the kitchen, "Well, how old will you be ten years from now if you *don't* go back to school and become a doctor?"

There is a stunned pause, then everyone bursts into laughter. In the end, Dave went back to school and today works as an ER doctor and a medical missionary.

When I finish the story, Brent says, "OK, I get it. But how does that apply?" Now it's time to pivot. If there is a risk he could take, a trade he could make, to live at a higher level, *will he take it?*

"Isn't full-time college around fourteen units per semester?" I say.

"That's a really full load, but yes."

"So, if you went back to school full-time, how long would it take to finish twenty-eight units?"

"Two semesters. A full school year."

"So if you started next month with fourteen units instead of three, you'd graduate next May, nine months away, right?"

"Right."

"Then you could take the state test next summer and at this time next year, you'd be a high school football coach, right?"

Silence. Thinking. Finally, Brent says, "I'd have to go back and live with my parents. My dad already offered to pay for school if I did. I'd have to do classes in the morning, then build fences the rest of the day and do my schoolwork at night. I'd probably only see Danielle just on Saturday nights and part of Sunday. Then back to studies Sunday night, hit Monday morning and repeat. Every week."

A pause. "Man, that would be painful. Brutal!"

So I ask, "*What amount of pain would you be willing to endure if you knew that at the end, you would have a career and a marriage to the girl of your dreams?*"

Silence.

I say, "Brent, seriously, you're a championship athlete. What could you not walk through if you knew what you fully desire was just nine months on the other side of the pain?"

He smiles—it hits. Brent grabs his Big Gulp and says, "Man, I gotta go call my dad! Paul, thanks. I'd be stupid not to do it."

"Hey, just a minute," I tell him. I remind him about Nehemiah and the prayer. I ask if he's ready to pray the prayer, accept responsibility for what he's done wrong, and ask God to rebuild the walls of his life. He has no hesitation.

We pray right at the table. As he stands to leave, he wipes his eyes, straightens his shoulders, and says, "Well, here we go. I hope God blesses this—because I'm going to work my tail off."

I sit there after he leaves, wondering what will come of it. Many men tell me they want to finish school, or study the Bible, or get a promotion, or change careers, or get their wives to love them, yet few are willing to invest more time, or give up their boat, or cancel their Netflix subscription, or skip buying the lift kit for their truck. Dumb stuff, but it keeps them from their dreams. They want to coast as pain-free as possible—all the time just prolonging the pain.

Nine months after meeting with Brent, my wife Judi and I had the privilege to attend his college graduation party. And, two weeks after his graduation, we witnessed his wedding to Danielle. Brent admits he wanted to quit every single week, and sometimes every single day. But he kept thinking about the prize, and it was worth paying the price. Today, he's coaching at one of the top-rated high schools in the nation.

As I was reading the final draft of this book, a text popped in. Brent. It may make this book sound like fiction—because the text said he was just voted Teacher of the Year.

He messaged, "You are wonderful and I owe so much to you and a conversation we had at Starbucks, if I remember right, where you said, 'How fast could you finish college if you absolutely had to and what would you do?' That talk changed my life! Thank you."

Brent did it. So can you. Don't quit. Pay the price, take the pain. Make tenacity your definition. Definitions drive decisions.

5

OPPORTUNITY

Your dream has a price. It will cost you sweat, effort, time, and discipline. Coach Paul "Bear" Bryant said, "It's not the will to win that matters—everyone has that. It's the will to prepare to win that matters."

My dad said, "Dreams are the substance of every great achievement." Many men have dreams—but very few actually do something about them. Your dreams won't just find you. They won't just happen. You have to make a real, concrete goal. You have to set yourself on fire. It must be something that pushes you, that wakes you up and gives you energy in the morning. Something that makes you come alive. A dream without a date is just a fantasy.

So often I've found myself wanting the dream, but without the pain. The highly quotable late, great boxer Muhammad Ali said, "The fight is won or lost far away from witnesses—behind the lines, in the gym and out there on the road, long before I dance under those lights."

Most men miss seizing opportunity because they won't pay the price and pain of preparation. People often quote the Hall of Fame player and coach John Wooden who said, "Failure to prepare is preparing to fail." My friend Robert Barriger says it this way, "Preparation is proof you expect something to happen."

Most people look for opportunity but don't *prepare* to be ready when the opportunity arrives. Opportunity comes to us all. Most failures aren't because of a lack of opportunity. Failures happen because opportunity tends to surprise us when we're unprepared.

My friend Wes was a young carpet salesman. He worked extra hours to save money for a down payment on a second house. He trusted God, knowing that if he honored the Lord by being generous, God would give him wisdom with his finances.

It took Wes two years to save up his first small down payment. He bought the house and rented it. Then, he worked more hours, bought another house, and rented that one. He did it again and again. He thought he was in the carpet business, until one day he woke up and realized he was in the real estate business. He was surprised by opportunity, but he had prepared himself.

After many years of learning the rental business, he took the increased value of all his homes and purchased an apartment complex. Then he bought another one. Then he built commercial buildings. Today, he funds missions projects around the world through the successful development company he's built. He has created a legacy of faith and funding that his family will carry on for generations.

Having faith in God is not believing in magic. Faith is trusting God for the wisdom to make right decisions in every area of your life. Faith is not a crutch—it's a foundation. Trusting God makes you faithful in what He has trusted you with.

Nehemiah was broken, crushed in his heart. But out of his brokenness, God gave him a dream. Nehemiah imagined *himself* as being the one to rebuild the city of Jerusalem. It sounded crazy. But he prayed over it. His prayer produced his passion. *Passion finds a way.*

After dreaming, Nehemiah moved into preparation. He doesn't say outright that he devised a plan, but we can see from his memoir that when he finally had the opportunity, he already had a plan.

Something had settled deep in the heart of Nehemiah. He began to look at the rebuilding of Jerusalem as part of his *destiny*. He began to dream of how it could be accomplished, of what needed to happen, what tools and resources were necessary.

Nehemiah was consumed every waking moment. It began to affect his demeanor. Finally, the king asked, "Hey bartender! What's wrong with you? You're always so upbeat. Why are you looking so down?"[1]

Nehemiah knew that talking directly to the king could get him killed. One wrong word and he was history. Kings of that day lived like gods. The people often thought they *were* gods—deity to be followed and obeyed. The king had the legal power of life and death. Because of that, people didn't want to see the king on a bad day. It could mean their death.

But someone had asked him about his passion. Here was the opportunity. Fear gripped Nehemiah, but he saw the opportunity and...boom. The passion of his heart, the preparations he'd made, the plans he'd conceived, all came out like a roaring river.

Nehemiah was ready for the opportunity. The right opportunity will reveal your true identity. Only the man who is ready makes use of it.

Nehemiah said, "The city of my fathers is destroyed. Jerusalem was once the capital of a great nation, the city that King David built. I have been distraught and dismayed. Something needs to happen to rebuild the walls and restore the city."[2]

Courage is the result of embraced destiny. Somewhere in the middle of fasting and prayer, Nehemiah had decided in his heart, "It's time for someone to speak up. If it's me, I'll do it."

Prayer and fasting builds boldness and courage.

The king spoke to Nehemiah, "What do you need, how can I help you?"

Nehemiah replied with a detailed plan.

But stop right here.

TOO OFTEN WE SHRINK OUR DREAMS TO MATCH OUR RESOURCES.

Nehemiah was a slave, a bartender. He wasn't a builder. He had no money and no real resources, and neither did his slave friends. He'd never done this before. And he'd never even seen the city he wanted to rebuild. It didn't look good.

But he had a dream and he knew a king.

So he wrote down a plan. He's a slave and a bartender...*but he wrote down a plan to rebuild the city of David*, the most important city ever built. He didn't just hope, he got ready.

Too often we shrink our dreams to match our resources. We limit our dreams to fit who we think we are when most of our identity has been based on what other people have said about us. Insane, but most of us do it.

How do you find your true identity? By losing yourself in friendship with Christ the King. By knowing God has a purpose for your life, and by finding it on your knees and in His Word. By doing what He says to do.

We can trust God to match His resources to the dreams He has given us.

Nehemiah would have heard or read the story of David and Goliath, the story of Gideon and his fleece. He would have prayed the prayers of Abraham and Moses. It increased the dimensions and capacity of his heart.

He was a bartender with his hands, but that's not who he was becoming in his heart. He was becoming the "Restorer of the Walls," the "Rescuer of His Family," and the "Leader of a Nation." His heart had come alive within the atmosphere of faith.

Who and where you are today is not who you will be tomorrow. If you have a dream, and you're willing to work on it, live toward it, set goals, make plans, prepare—your dream will change who you are. The size of your dream determines the dimensions of your heart.

Are you getting this? Nehemiah was a bartender, a slave—*but he had a plan!*

A business mentor once taught me this simple phrase, "Plan the work and work the plan." When we have a dream without a plan, we live with tension because we're in disagreement with ourselves. We know we should be living a larger life, but we see ourselves in light of who we are right here, right now, and we don't feel we have what it takes to act on the dream and make it a reality. We become stunted by our own lack of self-worth and the negative words of others. It's an identity issue.

> **THE SIZE OF YOUR DREAM DETERMINES THE DIMENSIONS OF YOUR HEART.**

Nehemiah created a detailed plan to rebuild a national capital a thousand miles away in a place he'd never been, in hopes of restoring the spirit of an entire nation.

People Nehemiah knew—slaves, relatives, coworkers—didn't believe he could pull it off, that he could make his dream happen. How *could* they believe it? He heard the negativity of his friends and lived with the negative talk in his own mind. But, his faith in God triumphed over his surroundings and circumstances.

The king said, "What do you need?" Nehemiah overcame his fears and told the king the plan.

The king's response? "Okay, let's get it done." Nehemiah had ignited something in the king. It was a big problem, a big challenge, a big dream, and the king rose to it. Campus Crusade founder Bill

Bright used to say, "Small dreams don't inflame the hearts of large people." This was a large dream—and the king wanted in.

"I'm behind you. I'll send money, letters of safe passage, requisitions for supplies, and an army," the king said. Then he added, "Nehemiah, I trust you, but I own you. You're my slave, so I trust that you will come back."

Nehemiah said in essence, "I'll be back." As he set out on the road to his dream, Nehemiah was still a slave. But it was no longer his identity. In the quiet of his slave quarters, he'd already grown beyond his circumstances—before he even started to live out his plan.

My friend Big Tommy Sirotnak was an unexpected person you wouldn't think would change the world for thousands of people. An energetic preacher in a football player's body, he told everyone he met about Jesus, quoting Scriptures and making quips like, "If you haven't had a head-on collision with the devil, maybe you're following him." His favorite quote was from my dad: "When you let other people create your world, they will always create it too small."

Tommy grew up as an oversized, feisty, neighborhood tough guy until he had a collision with Jesus Christ. He was accepted to the University of Southern California the year after their football team won the national championship. One day, Tommy decided just to walk into the famed Coach John Robinson's office and ask if he could play. Assistant Coach Marv Goux almost threw him out bodily. But Tommy kept returning and his persistence paid off.

At the first practice Tommy attended, all he could think about as he took the field were the negatives people had said to him. "Don't goof up!" "You'll never make it!" "No one has walked onto the USC team in twenty-five years!"

The first drill they gave Tommy was a one-on-one against 6'-7", 300-pound Keith Van Horne, who would go on to win Super Bowl XX playing for the Chicago Bears. The guy in the backfield Tommy was trying to tackle was future Hall-of-Famer Marcus Allen, who later would win the Heisman Trophy and a couple of Super Bowls, one as MVP.

That very first drill almost took Tommy out. Bloodied and bruised, with a broken nose, Tommy limped off the field dazed. Coach Goux smirked, but Tommy responded, "Coach, you're either going to have to kill me or kick me off this team, because I'm not giving up."

After thirty visits to the coach's office, and a few more broken noses, Tommy finally made the team as a walk-on. He was later named defensive captain along with Ronnie Lott, the future Hall-of-Famer and winner of four Super Bowls. Big Tommy didn't go on to have a career in professional football, but he had learned the lesson. He could not let others shape his world for him.

And Tommy never did. He became an unexpected evangelist, traveling the world, leading homeless people to Christ as well as politicians, professional athletes, and more. His ebullience and forceful personality attracted thousands of people to Christ. It all started when he overcame his identity crisis, recognized an opportunity, as remote as it was, and insisted on doing the hard work of achieving his dreams.

My heart was broken two weeks ago when I received a call about Tommy's sudden departure to be with the One he'd been talking about all these years. But the effects of his life have touched the world. The memorial service was populated by childhood neighbors, politicians, pro athletes, fraternity brothers, and friends from across the globe. Story after story was shared by people who met Jesus because of this crazy football player evangelist. When Tommy found his identity in Christ, his world became larger and he went home a champion.

6

GENEROSITY

The majestic Sierra Nevada mountains surrounding Lake Tahoe are a special place for me—from the time my parents took our family there when I was a young boy, to my first time on snow skis as a teenager, to hiking there with my own children. It's a place that lifts the spirit and enlarges the soul.

On a crisp, sunny day, Wes and I were having lunch near his cabin just outside of Truckee in the mountains surrounding Tahoe. We talked about life—the wins and losses, the opportunities and difficulties, and the goodness of God.

Wes spoke of helping orphans and giving financially to send the gospel around the world. Years earlier, he had learned that giving is the external evidence of love. Giving is the testimony of generosity. *"God so loved the world that He gave...."*[1]

The conversation reminded me of something the Lord had ministered to my heart a few weeks earlier. The Old Testament prophet Elisha had a group of understudy prophets that he mentored. One of his team died, leaving a widow and two sons. The deceased man's name isn't given in the biblical account. He was just one of the guys.

One day, the man's widow came to Elisha with a huge problem.[2] Her creditors were coming to foreclose on her home and—in the manner of those days—to take her boys into forced labor to pay off the debts. They could possibly spend years in slave labor. She was distraught.

She said, "They are coming soon to take my boys and my house. What can I do?"

Elisha said a curious thing. "What do you have in your house?" he asked her. Elisha knew that God could take what she had in her hand and make it part of a solution she just didn't see yet.

She replied, "Nothing...except for a flask of oil." There is always *something*. God can use any *something* you have. We think we have nothing. He takes the something we think is nothing and produces life.

Elisha said, "Borrow as many jars as you can, then go into your house and shut the door. Pour the olive oil into the jars until they are all full. Keep pouring." Olive oil was a valuable commodity in that era. This was a financial strategy.

She did as he said. Her obedience was about to bless her. Her sons went around the village and borrowed jars from as many as people as would lend them. Then the widow began to pour oil from the flask and...it didn't stop. Jar after jar was filled. The boys ran from home to home and brought more jars.

Then suddenly, she looked around. "Are there no more jars?" she said. "Hurry, bring me more jars. The oil is flowing. Our debts will all be paid and we will have money left to live on for years!"

Her sons replied, "There are no more jars we can borrow." And the oil stopped flowing.

This is a Middle Eastern village around 850 BC. Jars are what everyone used. It's like trying to find plastic baggies in your neighborhood. The village is full of jars, but the people stopped giving them.

When the people stopped giving, the oil stopped flowing.

Oil is often a biblical symbol of God's presence. When the oil was flowing, it was symbolic of God's generous nature. David and others were anointed with oil at pivotal times for specific tasks. Today we sometimes anoint people with oil to ask God to release His presence in their lives or situation. It is a symbolic gesture of the very real expression of God's loving and generous heart.

The prophet Isaiah said this about generosity:

> *The smooth tricks of scoundrels are evil.*
> *They plot crooked schemes.*
> *They lie to convict the poor,*
> *even when the cause of the poor is just.*
> *But generous people plan to do what is generous,*
> *and they stand firm in their generosity.*[3]

Generosity makes a man solid. It provides a strong foundation. Generosity is an outward manifestation of an inner character, one that is humble and unselfish. Generous men are stable men.

I told Wes my impression of the story of Elisha. Wes is a generous man. His generosity has built a strong foundation for his life—and for his family. He ordered us some after-sandwich coffees. I watched his kindness with the young waiter and I thought about that poor widow's sons. As I looked at Wes, I realized, here is a man who would have helped those boys find more jars. Because that's what generous people do.

GENEROUS MEN ARE STABLE MEN.

"*Generous people plan to do what is generous,*" Isaiah said.[4] Generous people keep the oil flowing. Generous people establish a strong foundation. Love for others is shown by a generous nature.

Build a strong foundation for your life—be a generous man.

7

TALK

On Sundays when I'm not traveling, I attend my son Brandon's church. One of the young leaders I see there is a tremendous servant and influencer for Jesus. Jonas is in the band or in the back, loving people, serving people, and creating an atmosphere of hope and healing. He's a vibrant follower of Jesus Christ. But Jonas once sat in a coffee shop and told me emphatically, "I'm only here because you said you'd meet me, but I want you to understand that I'll *never* go back to church."

Jonas was sick of the religious stuff, sick of people telling him what to do. But he did do one thing—he stopped talking long enough to listen. Then he acted. It wasn't just talk, he did something. He showed up. Then he kept showing up. And it's made him a man for others to emulate.

It was different for a friend of mine years ago. Straight out of film school, he went to work for a famous actor-turned-producer. He then decided he could do better and left that job, then another and another, always looking for the big hit. When we'd meet, he'd tell me about this project or that one—things that were just about to happen. It was all talk. He'd use the names of famous people to disguise the fact that he'd crashed and burned. His outside looked full, but his heart was vacant.

A lot of talk.

"Talk is cheap" because it doesn't cost the talker anything. But if you believe the talker, it can cost you everything.

In the New Testament, James reasoned in his open letter to Christians that you can talk about faith, you can talk about helping people, you can talk about living right—but until you *do* it, it's not real. If it is not accompanied by action, it is dead.[1]

My dad taught me, "If you don't write it down and make a plan, it doesn't exist."

To paraphrase business writer and entrepreneur Seth Godin, "Until you ship something, you haven't really created anything." To me that means, until you finish what you're doing and click "Send," you're just talking.

Words are creative. Words have power. Words can cut people. Words can build people up. Men have invested money based on someone's word, then lost it when that person didn't keep his word. Women have invested their hearts in the word of a man, then suffered broken hearts when he didn't keep his word.

We had a friend in Colorado who told his wife for years that he was going to change his destructive habits and lifestyle. He really meant it. But he didn't do it. For a few months everything would be great. Then he wouldn't keep his word. The drama would unfold again. Heart-felt promises would be made once more. The drama cycled on. After years of him not keeping his word, his wife wanted no part of it. A man's name is only as good as his word. When she no longer accepted his word, she no longer wanted his name. He was the only one surprised when she left.

My dad taught me that a man's word is what makes his name good. He would say, "God's name is good, because His word is good. He keeps His word, so we trust His name. As God's word is to Him, so a man's word should be to him. A man's word must be his bond."

When a man keeps his word, it makes him trustworthy. When a man keeps his word, it gives his children a good name. When a man keeps his word, he creates a wealth of honor. When a man keeps his word, his life is larger.

When you make a promise—keep it. In business, in relationships, with your family—when you keep your word, people will trust you. You will gain people's confidence and you will live with confidence. You'll begin to live like a real man.

Living small is when you talk about your dream but do nothing. You're dissatisfied and agree that you're living below what you were created for, but you just talk. You wonder why people don't take your word for things...but you're not trustworthy. Dad taught me that **trust is extended to the limit of truth and no further.**

My friend Jonathan lives in the nation with the largest Muslim population on earth. As a college student attending traditional churches, he grew discontented, much like Nehemiah. He saw that only 4 percent of the country were Christians and basically said, "Somebody ought to do something about this." Then he took action.

Together with two friends, they started a house church. It doubled, then doubled again, and now they co-pastor one of the world's largest churches. They've used our ministry's books and curriculum and mentored over a half-million men in the last fifteen years. And the Christian population problem? That "largest Muslim nation on earth," once 95 percent Muslim, now has over 30 percent followers of Jesus Christ. The capital city of that nation now has a Christian mayor.

"Somebody ought to do something" is talk. "I'm grabbing my buddies to make a plan" is action. Men talk because it's cheap...it costs them nothing. But action has a price.

Unexpected people change the world. Because they're willing to pay the price.

As a teenager, my friend Alex Mitala was dying of malaria in the jungle of his native Uganda when he had an encounter with Christ.

In the midst of the fever he heard the name "Jesus." Later at a chance encounter in a market he overheard people talking about who this Jesus was. The next day, sitting deep in the jungle in a clearing used as a church, he confirmed his decision to live for Christ. During the brutal reign of dictator Idi Amin, Alex was deported to Kenya because of his outspoken faith. But when Amin was gone, Alex was back.

Soon afterward, people around Alex started dropping dead from an unknown disease. They didn't know what it was. They called it "slim." People got sick, got thin, and then died. Uganda had become the world's epicenter for AIDS. It cut across the entire population. Soon, 75 percent of the military, 50 percent of the men, and 30 percent of the country overall were HIV positive. Houses were boarded up across the nation where entire families had died. The average life expectancy dropped to forty-five. It was a viral genocide.

Alex traveled to the United States in search of an answer. He heard my dad teach a message on sexual integrity that was titled, "The Glory of Virginity." Alex took a video with that message—a little plastic VHS case with tape inside—and started playing it in churches. In a polygamous country, with an economic base that depended on marriage alliances, the idea of virginity and marital fidelity was revolutionary. The average man had seven different sexual partners each year, whether married or unmarried, and children were routinely molested. It was an accepted part of culture—but the culture had to change.

Alex didn't just talk about it—he did something. He grabbed some friends and they started the "Glory of Virginity Movement," or GLOVIMO. Soon there were events in public squares, a national radio broadcast, public school programs, popular songs, and dramas to teach children to honor and protect their virginity—that it was their right. The result? Now, almost thirty years later, the rate of AIDS that once was over 30 percent has dropped to almost 6 percent.

When you stop just talking and move to aggressive action, stuff happens.

Don't talk about it—*do it.*

8

HEART

Why would the king notice if one of his slaves was feeling depressed or discouraged? Why would a king decide in an instant to go with a slave's plan? A man living as a deity in his own mind would not care about his bartender or his bartender's little plan. Or perhaps Nehemiah was in this place of honor as the king's bartender because something about him had attracted the king's advisors. Something in Nehemiah set him apart from the crowd, from a palace full of servants. Nehemiah was different, and it showed.

One of my best friends in high school was Greg, the greatest athlete in the school. He was the most popular player on the football team—the big man on campus. He embraced a heightened sense of who he was and that attracted people to him. I enjoyed hanging with Greg because everyone wanted to be around him…including the girls. We had fun. He was always loose, but when he was closing in on the next game, his focus became intense. He had influence because he won football games and championships.

Influence comes as a result of solving problems for people. Greg solved problems by making his school's dream of winning come true. Everywhere Jesus went, He healed the sick, cast out demons, and from that platform of influence, preached the kingdom. Jesus solved people's health issues, brought freedom to hearts in bondage, set people free from their negative past, then used His influence to talk about His Father and the kingdom.

WE BECOME WHAT IS IN OUR HEARTS.

Nehemiah had influence with the king because he had a spirit of excellence about him. It was attractive. People noticed him. He solved entertainment and safety issues for the king. He was good at his job. He was good with relationships. Even as a slave, he'd worked his way to the top—reporting directly to the king.

Then Nehemiah heard a bad report that stirred his heart, awakened his identity, and birthed a new dream. The vision of that dream was so intense it showed on his face. A man with a vision will always bleed that vision. It's so real that his sweat has vision in it.

We become what is in our hearts. Because of cell memory, our hearts have memory. Many ancient writers talked about people's hearts. They wrote, "God, I have put Your Word in my heart to keep from doing the wrong thing."[1] And, "Protect your heart, because from your heart comes the destiny of your life."[2]

What you have in your heart is what you will become. Your hands will end up doing what your heart has produced.

We can fake it. We can look good to deceive the world around us. But at our core, we *are* what is deep in our hearts. The hurts, wins, dreams, and desires that deeply define us will determine our destiny—because they determine our actions.

Behavior always follows belief.

What you do is based on what you believe. Belief is not just a function of your conscious mind. Beliefs reside deep inside you. Anger often is an outward response to an inner hurt that you just bumped up against. How often have we reacted to something or someone and been surprised by our own response?

A man without a vision for his life will listen to the last voice he heard. And then…life just happens. Sometimes we try to change, to get out of where we are. We work, try, make an effort, but here is the key: *A man without a vision for his future will always return to his past.*

The average person reads 200 words per minute. We speak on average 150 words per minute. But the self-talk in our minds is screaming along at 400 words per minute at the slowest. And it is negative by nature.

I heard my friend Pat Morley paraphrase a business axiom, "Your system of thinking is perfectly designed to achieve the results you are now getting."

Where you are right now is a result of what your thinking has been over the past few years. You are living the result today of your thought life yesterday.

What changes our behavior is a clear vision for our future. That's why the admonition of Jesus was so clever. He said, "Love God and love people. Everything else rises and falls on that."[3]

If you just *cannot* find your vision, you *can* let your vision find you. All you have to do is what Jesus said—love God and help people. We often find our path as we're helping someone else find theirs.

I've found that the easiest way to find your path is to discard the paths you don't want to travel. Make a list. Do the work.

Nate was a young man I watched grow up into a tremendous man of God. But a few years ago he was perplexed. He loved working as a carpenter and thought that might be his profession. But he also loved studying investing and how economics worked. He was young. We met for coffee, of course. We grabbed some mugs of single-origin brew and settled into a couple of chairs in the corner. "Nate, how old are you?" I asked.

"I'm twenty-four now."

"OK, great. So if you found your direction over the next twenty-four months and knew what you wanted to do with your career, would you be OK with finding that when you're twenty-six?"

"Well, if you say it that way, then yeah, I'd be OK with that. I just don't see how that happens. I have so many opportunities and there are so many directions it could go."

"Do you want to be an astronaut?"

"No," Nate laughed. "I guess I can cross that off the list."

"What would it look like, Nate, if you cross off everything you know you're not going to do...Navy Seal, pediatrician, and so on. Then, what if you took the job as a carpenter right now, committed to it for a year, and then see where you're at?"

Nate committed to being a carpenter. He loved the physical work, but the longer he worked at it, the more he discovered it didn't really fulfill him. The following year, he worked at a lumber company, thinking sales might be the spot. He checked in with me. Neither of these were "it." We kept praying, focusing, narrowing.

A friend of his was working at a brokerage firm and told him about an opening. He helped Nate get the job. Nate thrived. Today Nate is getting promotions, has married the girl of his dreams, is active in his church, and is loving life.

It has to do with hitting a target. My friend Will is a champion long shooter. His rifle is an amazing piece of engineering, and he can hit a target the size of a pie plate at a half-mile. He explained to me the concept of bracketing. When you sight your gun, you put the crosshairs on the target, then shoot and see where the bullet hits. Then you begin to bracket in the adjustments on your scope and rifle until you've put the crosshairs and the bullet right in the middle of the target. Everything in harmony. Everything in agreement. You have arrived at the perfect symmetry of weather, distance, atmosphere, and skill. You're on target.

Sight in your heart. Love God. Love people. It's bracketing. Find a way to serve someone and show your expression of love to God. Begin to discard the things that don't belong and stay focused on the target. When you get close, narrow your scope and shoot again.

God has a purpose for your life and a plan for mankind. Remember, you haven't missed His "perfect plan." You just need to find your purpose. Your heart will resonate when you do.

Most guys stop. They get used to their shots going somewhere unfulfilling and they just sit there, shooting blanks. Business leader Ross Perot said, "Most people give up just when they're about to achieve success."[4]

A parked car doesn't need directions. But when you're in motion, God can point you toward His fullest intention for your life. Open your heart. Love God, help people. Get in motion and God will guide you.

9

DAD

Your vision must be foremost in your heart. It must be in the front of your mind. Too often the issues of day-to-day life crowd out our vision, but our hearts change when we release the negative that crowds out the positive. We make the decision whether or not to have those negatives in our life. So, make different decisions. Habits are reshaped as they serve the new decisions. Just as light displaces darkness, habits are not broken, they are displaced.

Jesus said, "When you forgive others, you release from your heart the negative thoughts that are there. If you don't forgive others, you will retain the hurts and shame from things you've done or things that have happened to you."[1]

The key to having the right self-talk, to building a forward-moving life, to realizing your dreams, is this: your heart must be cleansed of negativity by filling it with positive content.

This is something I continually come back to. It's what Nehemiah did at the start of his prayer. He "repented out" all the negative thinking and behavior from his heart and acknowledged God, inviting him to fill up the empty places.

Nehemiah stood up as a man, repented of his failures, the failures of his entire family line, and even his nation. When he repented, it launched a process of heart-cleansing that only God can do. His vision became larger as his failures became smaller. The positive dreams of his heart displaced the negative context of his life.

You become the person you are in your heart. You become the story you tell yourself about yourself.

HABITS ARE NOT BROKEN, THEY ARE DISPLACED.

My friend Rafael pastors a thriving church in Florida. He grew up in Argentina in a dysfunctional home. We were playing golf—at least he was playing, I was hacking. We'd spent time together at conferences and meetings, but this was our first clear man-time. I asked him his story. He said, "My dad was a great guy, but he was a bad alcoholic who became more and more abusive. By the time I was twelve years old, my entire dream was to turn eighteen, beat up my dad, and leave the house."

"What happened?" I asked as I picked up my fourth putt on number 6.

"I was invited to a youth meeting at a local church when I was sixteen. I gave my life to Jesus and it was explosive. Christ cleaned up my heart, made my thoughts new, and gave me a vision to become a successful man. It was a massive turnaround."

"So you didn't beat up your dad?"

"Ha, no. He didn't change, but I changed. When I was eighteen, I told my dad I loved him, but I was leaving. I went to a Christian college, became a youth pastor, met my wife. Today, here we are living this amazing life helping others, building a tremendous church."

"What happened with your family? Your brothers and sisters?"

"I have one brother. Man, he's a mess."

"How?"

"Well, he's two years younger than me, so that makes him around forty-two now. But he's just like my dad. He's an alcoholic, he's abusive, he's angry and bitter. He's been married a few times. He's a total mess. It's so strange that he would become what he hated."

Standing on the tee of number 7, I reminded Rafael about Jesus' words, that if we forgive someone, the hurt is released from our hearts, but if we don't, it's retained in our hearts. We become what's in our hearts. His brother had held on to the negative.

WE BECOME WHAT IS RETAINED IN OUR HEARTS.

Rafael was deep in the Word, but he had never seen it this way. Now he saw the pattern in his own family. His brother never forgave his dad, so his unforgiveness actually bound the sins of his father to himself. Rafael had forgiven his dad, released it from his heart, and lived a free, fulfilled life. Forgiveness releases; unforgiveness binds. We become what is retained in our hearts. It's surprising how many men miss this, even accomplished leaders like Rafael.

I was in a northeastern city when I felt compelled to convey this truth to a group of men. At the end, I led them in a prayer, "God, I forgive my dad and I ask you to forgive me. I believe and trust Jesus. Help my heart to be cleaned from all this hurt, and the unforgiveness I've had toward him and others. Please allow me to live free. I release it from my life. And I ask You, God, to fill my life with the life of Jesus—*Amen!*"

It was an electrifying moment. You could sense the open hearts of the men. Some wept softly. Others grabbed a friend and hugged him, stifling sobs. Others were just silent, basking in the freedom the moment gave. For many, it was the first time in their lives they'd ever admitted what happened with their fathers, or with others.

But it wasn't the first time for a young father named Erik.

When the meeting ended, Erik approached me, his face beaming, eyes rimmed red, a plaid jacket hanging open, and a Bible and notebook in his hand. He asked if we could talk for a moment. He said, "That was just what I needed. My family life was totally a mess growing up. I've had addictions and now I'm in therapy, but my addictions messed up my marriage. My therapist told me to write four letters to my dad...that it would make me feel better. Well, I've only written two. But after today, I won't be needing them." He reached into a brown notebook he was carrying, ripped out some pages, and handed them to me.

"I was supposed to go over to his house tonight and give him these letters. But I'm not going to read all this anger to him. I'm going to tell him straight up that I forgive him. I forgive what he did to me and mom. I'm going to tell him I love him. No matter what." His tears started again. We hugged. Prayed together. I hit him in the shoulder, then his friend standing nearby grabbed him. They were going together to see his dad. Erik left that room a free man.

On the plane the next morning, I took his letters out of my backpack. You could see the pain in the scrawled handwriting covering the pages. Here's some of what Erik had written to his father:

Dear disconnected, self-centered, and emotionally robbed Dad,

I feel you live in a world of your own creating. You try to reach out for interaction but no one is there. You pushed us away at a young age then expect us to be there in our adult years.

I think back to the times I needed a dad, when I was being told I was doing it wrong, when I was learning to shave, or when I was using sex to mask my pain. Instead, I was supplied with a tyrant, building a kingdom suited for himself.

I never asked you to be perfect, just to interact or just to sit with me for five minutes without the TV or phone involved. Why is loving me so hard? Why is my love too high of a price but my self-esteem so cheap? Why won't you go fishing or camping with me? I just wish you would be a full dad, not just a good-enough dad.

Letter two was full of more pain:

Dear George,

I am writing you in a more formal manner. I don't feel you warrant the title "Dad." While I was a child, you were disconnected, a bully, and shaped my family to only serve you.

You made me feel small and insignificant. You hurt my feelings with no remorse. You are a man with low character and no regard for others. This selfishness has made boundaries that made you unable to love or be loved.

I have decided for my family, I will not spend my time trying to chase the idea of you. I have my own family and they need me to be the father I was never taught to be. Goodbye.

I could hardly stop the tears as I read his anguish. How many men feel this way? But now—Erik was being healed. These letters were torn out of his binder and out of his heart. He was becoming a new, free man. Forgiveness has massive power.

Maybe you have harbored the same feelings in your own heart. You can be free today just like Erik. You don't have live with your story framed by unforgiveness, bitterness, and pain. Until your heart is clean of the toxicity of dysfunction, you'll never become what you were designed by God to be.

It may be your dad, might be an ex-business partner, or former wife or girlfriend. You've found yourself covered up with issues because you're acting out what's in your heart. Get rid of it. Get set free, forgive, and get released.

Some big, husky mountain man in Montana walked up to me on a Sunday morning at the close of the service. Big hands, strong handshake. "Thank you for yesterday," he blurted.

"What happened yesterday?" We'd held a regional men's conference, but I didn't remember seeing him.

He said, "I didn't know who my dad was until I was twenty years old. And I was always upset about it. When I did meet him when I was twenty, he looked me straight in the eye and said, 'Get the %*&# out of here. I don't want anything to do with you or your momma.' I've hated him for forty years. Every relationship in my life has been a mess. Yesterday, I discovered why. Unforgiveness."

I shoved his shoulder. His eyes were getting misty, and he didn't mask it. He put it all out there, straight up.

"Yesterday, for the first time in my life, I forgave my dad. And I meant it. I owned it, I dealt with it—and I forgave him. Today I woke up, and for the first time in my life, I felt like a free man. So, thanks."

We hit each other again, shook hands, hugged. He turned and walked away. No chitchat. Done. Boom.

Free. You can be, too. Forgive.

10
ARMY

I moved to Santa Cruz, California, "Surf City USA," at the beginning of my teenage years. I hadn't grown up surfing, and I didn't want to learn in front of the hip surf crowd at Cowells or Pleasure Point. Didn't want to look like a geek. So my friend Bob and I cut school, "borrowed" his mom's car, took some surfboards from the houses of friends, and drove up the coast to a deserted beach. We were going to learn how to surf.

We made a couple of mistakes right at the start. We didn't get training or ask anyone how to surf. We were going to figure it out ourselves. And, we didn't tell anyone where we were going.

Without knowing the ocean at all, the ebb and flow of the tides, the movement of the currents, or the danger of riptides, we enthusiastically pushed off into the waves. What we didn't see was a north-to-south current that began pushing us into a rock shelf. A reef that had been hidden was uncovered by the tide going out, and it was dangerous. We paddled away furiously. The receding tide made the waves larger, so we paddled the surfboards further away from shore. Now we were scared.

A couple of old men without clothes appeared on what we'd thought was a deserted beach and yelled, "ARE YOU GUYS OK?"

We freaked out. We were either going to die by getting smashed on the rocks or by getting slashed by some naked stalkers from an asylum.

We yelled back, "YEAH, WE'RE GOOD."

Desperate, tired, and seriously thinking we were about to die, Bob and I finally got off our boards and pushed them into some large waves. They crashed against the rocks, but at least they were headed to the shore. Bob and I then swam what seemed like a mile, but was likely a tenth of that, and finally reached the beach. We were safe. By then, even the naked guys were gone. We lay on our backs and thanked God. Then we kissed the sand, recovered the boards, and promised each other we would never, ever tell this story to anyone. Ever. (Sorry, Bob.)

I've gained a bit of wisdom since then.

First, when you start something, learn from the people who know how to do it.

Second, if you don't know those people, go find them. Experts enjoy giving wisdom and counsel to people who will listen and are eager to learn.

There are people around you who know what you need even if you don't. The best question in business is, "What do you know that I don't know, that I should know?" The most successful men in the world ask that question.

Third, if you're going to learn to surf, never surf with someone who doesn't know how. It's the same as surfing alone. And that's the cardinal rule of surfing...never surf alone.

Nehemiah didn't know he needed an army, but the king knew. He sent an army with Nehemiah. When the king caught the passion of Nehemiah's vision, he became involved. The king had been to war. He had built large projects. He had seen treachery. He knew the ways of evil men. He knew what Nehemiah needed, so he sent a captain and a small army.

An army wasn't in Nehemiah's plan. But Nehemiah was humble enough to adjust his plan to accommodate the army. He didn't know—but the king did.

————————

Men have to find out what they don't know from others. It takes humility. Tom Mohler lives in Sonora, California, a mountain town in Mother Lode country where my family lived when I was a small child. Tom wanted to reignite a failing church plant in that rugged territory. He prayed and worked at it, but couldn't get it off the ground.

One day as he was ministering, he realized there were only three men in the church building—and he was one of them. He knew he needed to start "majoring in men" to build the church. Tom contacted the Christian Men's Network and learned about a program that generally results in a 20 percent church increase across the board. Our guys coached him, which is what they love to do. Tom did exactly what the coaches and the manual said to do. After a year, he sent me a one-line email, "We've grown 30%." By the end of the second year, the church had doubled. The next year, more growth, and as I write, the church is on track to double again.

Tom didn't go it alone. He asked for directions.

My friend Bill has built his business by being willing to ask people what they know that he doesn't. You never know who is going to give you the answer you need. One year after he acquired a new business and started shutting down nonproducing departments, he conducted exit interviews. A woman sat in front of him who he knew they would have to let go regardless of what she said.

"What do you know that I don't know?" he asked.

She replied, "I know that the previous owner never marketed my product line properly, but if we did, it would be huge. I know that if you keep me on, and give me ninety days to do it my way, I'll show you." Bill was surprised. He talked it over with his partners, and they gave this nondescript manager a ninety-day grace period.

Her methods worked. Today, she's still working for them and taking home ten times more than she'd ever earned before, just in commissions alone. And Bill's business has gone global.

I sat at coffee with a man whom I had just met through some mutual friends. We began to talk about his story and his experience in planting churches. Somehow his story rang a bell, and I asked him, "Hey, are you that guy?" He was. He'd been written about in Rick Warren's great book, *The Purpose Driven Church*. He was the pastor who went to Rick for counsel. Rick told him, in essence, that he was in the wrong culture. If he'd move a few miles away, his church would explode. The man didn't believe it at first but out of desperation finally followed Rick's advice. It worked.

VISION IN ACTION ATTRACTS ANSWERS TO NEEDS.

"I'm the guy!" the pastor said. "It happened exactly the way Rick wrote it. 'If you'll move three miles, it will change everything.' And it did."

Ask the experts. Every man needs an army.

Vision in action attracts answers to needs. A vision acted on builds hope in people. Where there is *no* vision, people lose heart. Making a decision to act brings life to a project or dream. Making a decision to act on your dream will spark passion in you—and in the people you need.

Teddy Roosevelt is said to have remarked: "At the moment you face a great obstacle, the most important thing is to make the right decision. The second most important thing is to just make a decision."

Decisions create energy. Indecision produces inertia, the loss of momentum and passivity. Decisive men build strength, indecisive men become weak.

Throughout history, you'll see that until a vision is acted on, the provision doesn't show up. When Nehemiah began to release his vision—declare his dream, act in boldness and faith—the provision he needed became available.

———————

I hadn't seen much of Jacob, a great young guy who was launching a career in engineering at a nearby firm. We managed to grab a quick lunch one day. With coffee. As I listened to his situation, I said, "Jacob, God has an army."

"What does that mean?"

"It means that God has provided you with the power of the Holy Spirit." I pulled out my phone and flipped through my Bible. "He has promised never to leave you on your own. He's always there. He has your back. My wife's favorite Scripture is from the book of Hebrews. It's best in the *Amplified* translation because it gives us the underlying meaning. Here it is. Read it out loud."

Jacob read, "...*[God] Himself has said, I will not in any way fail you nor give you up nor leave you without support. [I will] not, [I will] not, [I will] not in any degree leave you helpless nor forsake nor let [you] down (relax My hold on you)! [Assuredly not!]*"[1]

He looked at me and said, "Wow!" Then he read it again a few times, his engineering mind clicking into gear.

I explained. In the passage, a phrase is repeated three times—"*I will not, I will not, I will not.*" It's ancient legal language meaning that this is an unbreakable agreement. It's even stronger than a contract. It's a covenant. People back then understood it. When men would make an agreement, they would stand in front of the city elders and state it three times. No mistakes. Repeat it three times. Then it became binding.

It doesn't matter if you're a young engineer starting out, a middle-aged school bus driver, a former addict of some kind, or a skateboarding teenager. God has given you a covenant.

As a covenant, it can never be changed or altered in any way. A contract between people can be revised, but a covenant between God and man is done. Complete. Finished. In stone. The way it's going to stand from now on.

God is not going to leave you helpless. He knows what you need, and He has everything you need. Just start asking.

Walk like God's got your back. Because He does.

11

QUALIFIED

"I had my shot. It's gone." I've heard the same lament from hundreds of men during forty years of mentoring and coaching. It always sounds the same because it's from the same source. The enemy has convinced them of the same old tired lie: "You can't do it. It's too late."

The lie cuts two ways. Either, you're *not* qualified, no one would ever want you, and you're stupid for thinking you could do it. Or, you're *dis*qualified, you made bad choices, you're out.

That lie becomes the identifying factor that limits a man's life. At the root of the lie is a wrong picture of God. It paints God to be like a man who judges solely on actions or outward attributes, basing His measure of a man on performance or good qualities.

The lie is an accusation against you, and it's also an accusation against God. It accuses Him of not being able to do what He says He can do. That His power is limited. That He can be manipulated—that doing enough good things will qualify you for God's blessing, but doing wrong things will disqualify you.

Satan's first accusation against God was that God was a liar. *"Did God really say…?"*[1] he said to Eve in the garden, to manipulate her heart. His intent was to cast doubt on God's word, to lower God to his level, to become equal with him. The enemy always tries to lower men to an inferior level by manipulation and accusation.

The enemy is a liar. He is full of dung (to use King James English).

A few weeks ago, I met Michael Phillips for the first time. Michael was disqualified by education, by the police, by himself, and by his circumstances. Yet he is now a tremendous success. Michael grew up in the inner city of Baltimore where, as he puts it, young black men learned to jump high to get ahead in life. He excelled and received letters from dozens of colleges offering a basketball scholarship. The future finally looked good.

His dad had died when Michael was only twelve. Dad had been a pastor, working two jobs to support his family while he ministered. When his dad died, Michael's mom took over the church that was housed in a historic, shuttered high school. After the funeral, Michael kicked around the neighborhood, growing up like most of his friends, without a strong male presence. But finally, Michael caught a break. Basketball was his ticket.

But that September, just after arriving at college, a car accident thrashed his leg. Michael never played in even one college game. Instead, he hid in the dorm, drowning himself in alcohol and drugs. The school invited him to stop doing so in their dorm, and he found himself back home—just like all the guys who didn't make it in school or sports. He joined forces with some of them and started dealing drugs. To make additional money, Michael found he was pretty good at financial fraud. Soon, he had a fast car. He had money. He had made it after all.

The bust came early one morning, and Michael was thrown in jail. Four days later, a judge called for Michael. In the judge's chambers, a lawyer Michael had never met sat eyeing him. The judge said, "This lawyer found out you were accepted at more than twenty colleges. So, I'm giving you a choice—jail or college." Michael squirmed. *Here we go....* "College," he said.

The lawyer held out a paper to the judge, which happened to be the first paper the lawyer pulled out of a box when he visited Michael's mother. The judge looked it over and said, "Okay, you're going here." The paper was an acceptance letter from Oral Roberts University. Michael's squirm turned into a spasm. A Christian school was the last place on earth he wanted to go to.

Michael didn't want anything to do with God, but at ORU he had a divine encounter. Michael stopped believing a limiting lie and started believing what God's Word said about him. After college, he went into sales. He married a brilliant woman who was working on her PhD. They had two children. Life was good. Then one night, God spoke to Michael's heart to return to the place where he'd grown up. Once again, it was the last place on earth....

Together with his wife, they moved their young family back to Baltimore and walked into what had first been his father's, then his mother's, and now his church, a place filled with so many painful memories. On the Friday before the first Sunday when Michael was going to take the pulpit, a constable showed up with a foreclosure notice. That was just the start. One terrible setback was followed by a miracle, followed by hard work, followed by other setbacks, over and over, year after year.

One day, the largest building developer in Baltimore came to watch his grandson play soccer in the park behind Michael's church. After the game, the man went to check out the large decrepit building he'd never before noticed. He met Michael, and learned what the building *was* and also what it *could be*. He introduced Michael to a financier. The three men joined forces. Currently, they have raised tens of millions of dollars, refurbished the building, launched a school, laid plans for a grocery store and for more schools, and are meeting the needs of the people in the neighborhood. Drug dealers have moved out. The congregation is encouraged, energetic, and growing.

Michael was disqualified by every measure on earth. But he was never disqualified to God. Growing up without any encouragement or reinforcement of who he was, what he was good at, or who he could be, he just drifted. Today, he sits on boards that make large decisions regarding education, government, health care, and more. His wife with an earned PhD presides over a clinic. His daughter is excelling in dance and music, and his son was just accepted to Harvard.

Other people disqualified Michael. Michael disqualified Michael. But God did not disqualify Michael. His repentance qualified him, God's grace empowered him, and his faithfulness sustains him. God put Michael right back into his destiny where he is now fulfilling his calling.

Repentance always renews and restores. Repentance reconciles us to God. Repentance is the pivot point between ruin and reconciliation. Repentance defines a man.

The message of Jesus Christ is that He pre-qualified each of us through repentance.

As you read, understand—you *cannot* define yourself based on one mistake—or a few mistakes, even big ones. When God forgives you, you're no longer defined by your past. You're defined by your tomorrows. Jesus never defined a man by his past, He always called men into their future. Every day you walk with Christ, you become more and more of who you really are, your true identity.

I am not defined as a man by the things I struggle with.
I am defined as a man by the fact that I am a passionate pursuer of the power of God's presence.

That's it. Not qualified by good works. Not disqualified by anything that has happened to you—or anything you've ever done. When we repent and ask God to clean our hearts, it's done.

Paul wrote in a letter to a church in ancient Corinth, "When you become a follower of Jesus Christ, all the old things pass away and all your life becomes new. You are a spiritual new creation, because of Jesus Christ."[2] You are no longer that old person, that's not your story. You are...

New. Fresh. Redeemed. Qualified.

12

FOCUS

When Nehemiah arrived in Jerusalem, it was worse than he had expected. The brokenness and destruction became fully evident as they rode over the last ridge a few miles from the city. Abandoned tools lay discarded alongside fallen arches and tumbled bricks. Goats tore at weeds growing up from the tattered stalls that once held a bustling marketplace. Homes that had held families and a vibrant community were covered with desert sand and tumbleweeds. Thistles poked through what was left of the streets. It wasn't just chaotic, it was total defeat. A spirit of fear filled the atmosphere. People were scratching out a living in isolated, ragged tents along the valley outside the east gate.

It was time to move into action. His emotions told him to get things going—*now*. But Nehemiah paused. Rather than spring immediately into furious action, he did something too many men fail to do. He took a breath. He quieted his spirit. He focused his heart. Focus is not about greater intensity. It's about greater intentionality.

Nehemiah gathered up the passion in his heart and got still. He got away from the voices speaking negative reports to him. Understand, your heart will lean in the direction of the voices you listen to. The bent of your life influences your decisions. Your decisions direct your life. That's why reading the Bible is so important. Your heart leans into God when you're reading His Word.

What you receive into your heart will lead you into your purpose. Then you act on that deep-felt purpose.

The enemy lives in chaos. Noise. Confusion. Turmoil.

Your mind can have 40 thoughts per second multiplied by 88,400 seconds in a day.

Your brain has 100 billion neurons that are making 100 trillion connections every day.

FOCUS!

Nehemiah got quiet. Our hearts thrive when we hear the measured, peaceful, wise, and gracious voice of God.

Nehemiah did what Mary did when the angel told her she was to conceive the son of Almighty God. She kept the vision deep in her heart and didn't tell anyone other than Joseph and her cousin Elizabeth. The apostle Luke writes that after the birth of Christ, she again pondered what was happening in her heart. We need some men who will ponder. (That means, *stop and think about it*.) Mary got her heart focused toward the task ahead of her, raising the Son of God.

> **FOCUS IS NOT ABOUT GREATER INTENSITY. IT'S ABOUT GREATER INTENTIONALITY.**

Nehemiah didn't tell anyone his plans when he arrived in Jerusalem. He didn't pull up with his army and read off a major proclamation: "I'm here to rebuild the wall, people!" He paused for three days, a measurement of time that often in the Bible signifies something has been completed that is beyond the scope of man to manipulate. Nehemiah rested, then he went out late at night and surveyed the walls. None of the residents knew what he was doing. In the quiet he found his focus.

Why was he so quiet about something he was so passionate about?

Because people are negative by nature. It is easy to disparage. We tend toward the negative. It is easy to say why something can't be done or it's impossible or it's never been done before or we've tried it and it doesn't work. That's why negative advertising is so pervasive in political campaigns—it works.

———————

My wife Judi and I have a friend, Jan, who was looking for a new home in the mountains. She had surveyed the neighborhoods and chose an area of custom homes with beautiful views. She saw one online that looked interesting. The realtor discouraged her. "That house has been on the market for almost three years. They keep lowering the price. No one who goes there likes it. I wouldn't waste the time."

Jan went to see other houses, but nothing clicked. Finally, she convinced the realtor to show her the house that no one wanted. Built by an artist, it was beautifully constructed—loaded with extras inside and making the most of the mountain views outside. Jan's heart quickened until she rounded a corner into the kitchen. Her heart sank to see how low and dark the kitchen was, with a single, small window. Jan knew then why it didn't sell. No woman wanted to pay the price of a custom home and get a dark, depressing kitchen area. It made everything seem dark and closed in.

Jan went home and focused on the problem. She had a vision for where she would live and that house fit her vision, but it was flawed. She prayed, got alone, got quiet. She meditated on the problem, focused, then she saw what no one else saw.

She and her husband Bill met with the builder and asked, "What is above the kitchen ceiling?" The builder scratched his head and said, "Well, nothing really, it's just a vacant space." So Bill and Jan purchased the house no one wanted at a below-market price. The first thing Jan did was have the builder come back and raise the kitchen ceiling, enlarge the windows over the sink and open up the walls. Opening up the room to the spectacular views changed the atmosphere of the entire home. Bill and Jan moved in, started getting to know people, and invited the neighbors over. More than one asked in stunned tones, "It's beautiful! We loved the location, why didn't we buy this?"

Vision and imagination happen in the quiet.

A hundred people could have bought that home, but no one else saw what Jan saw. She had vision that was focused. She pondered the problem until God gave her the solution.

———

I like to go fishing. It's something I've enjoyed all my life but I have just recently discovered it helps me decompress, so Judi encourages me to do it often. As I've fished more, I've learned about the dynamic tension of a rod, the attraction of certain bait, lures, or flies for particular fish. I've had men coach me on casting, drag tension, and patterns of why and how fish strike. I've watched YouTube videos of fishing tips and gone with guides to gold-medal lakes and streams. But what I've learned is that at the end of the day, fishing really comes down to the person holding the rod.

To fish well requires total focus, to the full exclusion of everything else around. At any moment, I have to be ready for a strike on the bait. Quiet. Expecting. Focused.

Life is not just about the information or training we get. Yes, we all need help, training, mentoring. But afterward, it's all execution. It's focusing our will and desires in the direction of the intended result. You can be taught by a great basketball coach, but the results depend on whether you execute what you've been taught on the court. Whether we are building a wall, buying a house, or casting for a fish, it's about disciplining our lives for the results we want. When you intentionally focus on the things you're dreaming about—*something is going to happen.*

Focus propels vision forward. Like rocket fuel.

There is an enemy trying to invade your thought life with the mundane. The trivial. The negative. Trash. He goes after you night and day. Vision is forged in the discipline of extracting yourself from the unnecessary.

You need to be like Nehemiah and take time to get away. Get quiet. Find peace. It might be late at night on your porch, or early in the morning before the kids wake up. It might be at a lake or in the mountains or on a drive or on the train. Wherever. *Find the quiet.*

> ## VISION IS FORGED IN THE DISCIPLINE OF EXTRACTING YOURSELF FROM THE UNNECESSARY.

You do not have to look for the presence of God. When you pause to focus on Him, His presence will find you. He promises He is there—*always*. Silence, quiet, reading His Word, meditating, thinking deeply, all just open your heart to His presence that was there all the time.

Once you've made the decision, then come out with power and *crank it up*!

It has been said, "You cannot fight hard unless you believe you are fighting to win."

The world, the enemy, people around you will all find reasons not to get it done. You must make the choice in the quiet of your alone time with God. Then go for it with reckless abandon…because you've found your purpose.

Success is the result of constancy of purpose.

> Remember that in a race everyone runs, but only one person gets the prize. You also must run in such a way that you will win. All athletes practice strict self-control. They do it to win a prize that will fade away, but we do it for an eternal prize. So I run straight to the goal with purpose in every step. I am not like a boxer who misses his punches. I discipline my body like an athlete, training it to do what it should.

Otherwise, I fear that after preaching to others I myself might be disqualified.[1]

The life of Jesus Christ in the heart of a man will create dreams and desires that are different than those we had in a life without God. Christ's life creates new targets that change the trajectory of our lives. Our priorities shift. It's not just about the stuff everyone else seems to long for—and the world tells us we must have. Christ's life in us brings an appetite for the real things—for the purpose He placed within us when He created us.

The dynamic power of the life of Jesus Christ in the heart of a man is the birth of purpose. His Spirit helps us focus our lives on that true *purpose*.

The strength of Jesus living on earth as a man was His focus, the intentionality of His life. There was no wasted motion. No wasted moment. Even when He was just kicking back with His friends. Even the times He got away from crowds. He always had a focused purpose. It helped Him quiet His humanity and the turmoil around Him.

People with a vision accomplish great things. They're willing to work for it. Nehemiah wasn't on some sort of "find myself" grand adventure. He had a vision, a purpose, and he was there to get the work done. It was in him.

Sun Tzu, the consummate military strategist, said, "One who is confused in his purpose, cannot respond to his enemy."[2]

––––––––––––

Have you ever noticed at a gym how many of the men just sort of go through the motions? They're talking to friends, then wander over to a different machine or weight area, a little off-focus.

Now, what if you told that unfocused guy that he was going to fight Floyd Mayweather next month? Do you think it would change his workout routine?

Most men live their lives without a clear vision or purpose. So they lose energy as they age, sometimes even in their early twenties. Life just winds down to a nice little path from the recliner to the refrigerator, from the garage to the parking lot. Repeat. Day after day.

Focus gives a man five things:

Energy

Boldness

Tenacity

Creativity

Strategy

Columbus sailed from Spain to the edge of unknown seas because he was focused on the prize, the target, his vision. He sailed from August 3 to October 11. His crew became uneasy, dismayed, ready to rebel, to sail back home.

Columbus wrote in his journal, "Would have lost hope, if I did not believe I was going the right direction."

The ancient prophet Hosea said about the men in his culture, "*They look everywhere except to heaven, to the Most High God. They are like a crooked bow that always misses targets.*"[3]

A man with a vision from God won't stop. He won't listen to the negative people around him. He infuses his life with the Word of God, with strategies, with hope, with stories of great men and heroes. He cannot be dissuaded. He will not be distracted. And he surrounds himself with men who have the same spirit.

My friend Joel had an encounter with God at age eighteen. He began to plan, think about, go after, and put himself in position to be a minister of the gospel. He dreamed about it, wrote ideas and sermons on scraps of paper and the backs of napkins. It was his passion. What happened? Bad stuff. Joel attended a Bible school with guys who weren't serious. He was discouraged by leaders he admired. He graduated and shuffled through a few different jobs. He sat on the sidelines. Finally, he was relegated to driving the airport van for a television ministry.

But, driving that van, picking up people at the airport, he wouldn't let go of his dream. He began to ask the leaders he served about their lives, their preparation, their dreams. Godly leaders from around the world began to teach Joel, to impart to him their wisdom, to teach him about capacity, faith, endurance, and becoming a servant-leader. Joel listened and learned. He embraced it. He saw it. He wouldn't let go.

Today Joel is one of the leading authors and evangelists in the world. How? With all his dreaming and passion, he would not let go of his vision. He stayed focused. His focus on Christ and serving others brought life to his vision…and his vision to life.

He was just a van driver, but today he and his wife lead a ministry that influences millions. Unexpected people change the world.

––––––––––

If it's God's purpose for you, then it must become *your* purpose and *your* passion. God will give you strength but you have to do the lifting. That's why you need the place of quiet. Get away and focus deeply, or your dream will not happen.

I've met countless men around the world who have told me about their dreams, their desires, what they want to do. My question is always, *"What have you done to start the process?"*

Dreamers make the world beautiful but visionaries change the course of history.

Nehemiah went out late at night. After three days of getting rested and acclimated, he went out when no one was around. Took a few of his assistants and surveyed the entire city. The local men were asleep. They had been for ninety-two years.

After seeing the city. After getting into a place of clarity and perspective. After focusing his heart and spirit. The next day— Nehemiah made his declaration.

"We are rebuilding Jerusalem!"

Then he started…and was unstoppable.

13

DISAPPOINTMENT

"You don't understand."

"What don't I understand?" I said to Jeremy as we walked out of another powerful Sunday meeting at church.

His shoulders were down. He was pensive, quiet.

"You know, I'm all in. Going to church and all. It gets me pumped up, but then I crash and burn before I'm even out of the building. I feel like I can do it, but I feel like a failure, too."

"What gets you feeling like a failure?"

Jeremy got quiet. A sharp twenty-something young man with tremendous talent, he'd never had a dad who mentored him, or even spent time with him. He had a void. The enemy tried to fill it with a negative identity. Whenever we touched something deep, he would get quiet.

His disappointments in life, in his dad, in others, and mostly in himself had created a briar patch of emotional hurts that he couldn't get untangled from. His disappointments had become his identity.

Disappointment is what David wrote about in the twenty-third psalm: "...*the valley of the shadow of death.*" It's not the valley of *death*, it's a *shadow* of death. Disappointments are not death, but they have the shadow of death on them. When we live like the shadows contain certain death we empower the darkness.

The apostle Paul told his young pupil, Timothy, "God did not give you a spirit of fear, but power, love, and wisdom!"[1]

DISAPPOINTMENTS ARE NOT DEATH, BUT THEY HAVE THE SHADOW OF DEATH ON THEM.

Jeremy and I rode the mountain bike trails around Lake Grapevine later that week. As we stopped for some water and a GU Gel energy hit, I talked with him about the power of forgiveness and the path to freedom. Here's what was interesting: what Jeremy had done is forgive others, but never himself. That day in a clearing beside the lake, Jeremy said a small prayer and had a huge encounter. When Jeremy forgave himself, based on the promises of God, something broke open. He walked out of the shadows.

As he did, he also forgave his teachers, bosses, friends, the school, his truck—I mean, anything he thought of, he just got it out. Like a pipe-cleaning auger, the Holy Spirit cleared out the disappointment that had fouled his inner filter. Jeremy humbled himself, forgave himself, and freed his ability to hear truth without his heart being clogged with disappointment. The Bible says Jesus came as the light. In Christ there are no shadows.

Jeremy *had* been camping in the valley of the shadow of death. But he got up and walked out.

Don't fear the shadows.

───────

When Nehemiah arrived in Jerusalem, he discovered hundreds of people living in the decrepit area. Some had taken the stones from the broken walls and built homes for themselves. To them, the wall's stones were just rocks. The desolate city was in disarray. It reeked of the stench of disappointment and despair.

Nehemiah's plan didn't including bringing workers with him because there were enough there already. So why hadn't they rebuilt? The walls had been decaying for over ninety years. The people had cried, moaned, and complained about it...*but no one had done anything about it.*

Perhaps this is why Nehemiah had been so distraught when he heard about the ruins back in Persia. He had expected to hear that the men who had said they would rebuild were actually working on it. But nothing had been done. The decay just worsened each day without anyone stepping in to help.

Nehemiah felt the agonizing sting of disappointment. He tasted the bitterness of its poison. He was walking through the shadow of death. It was pervasive.

> **Disappointment is not based on what you find,**
> **but on what you expected to find.**
> **Disappointment is not based on where you are,**
> **but on where you expected to be.**

If you expected by now to be the manager of a company, but the reality is that you're working in the warehouse—you're disappointed. If you expected your marriage to last, but the reality is that it failed—you're disappointed. If you thought you would be done with school already, but the reality is you're far from finishing—you're disappointed.

The level of disappointment in a man's life is based on the gap between expectation and reality.

The greater the gap between expectation and reality, the greater the degree of disappointment. That gap becomes your valley, shadowed by death.

Disappointment, when held on to, becomes discouragement. A discouraged man stops dealing in reality, because reality is just too painful. He loses hope. So in his discouragement, he disconnects. His disconnection leads to depression, where he's no longer trying to be positive. And finally the enemy wins and his dreams die.

The pattern is: disappointment, discouragement, disconnection, depression, death.

Jeremy had allowed his disappointment to define him. That embrace of a false definition had him squeezed into a pattern toward death. Only God can rescue a man from the vice-grip of that pattern.

Disappointment comes to every man's life. But the effect of disappointment is polarized—either lean toward God, or lean toward discouragement. You choose.

Jesus came to be the way—out of the valley. He is the way, there is no other.

———

Jedaiah had lived next to the broken walls of Jerusalem his entire life. He passed them every day. As a small boy he threw rocks and played on the piles. He ran across the shaky bulwarks until one of the moms in the neighborhood screamed at him and his friends to get down. Sometimes he wondered why it never was fixed. But it made for great climbing.

As Jedaiah grew older, he accepted the negative assessment he heard from his father and neighbors. It's too costly to repair. We don't have the tools necessary. We'll never finish it. It's too far gone and may not be able to be rebuilt. A hundred reasons not to start. Some legitimate ones, like "our enemies will come and kill us for rebuilding it."

For over ninety years the excuses grew larger as the once proud city decayed into dust.

———

In 1974, a coastal city in Cyprus was abandoned during the Turkish invasion. Varosha was the one of the most beautiful resort cities in the world, a party place for the very rich. To this day, it is a city full of high rises and neighborhoods, car dealerships and markets. But—they are all abandoned. During the war years, the military put a fence around the city. Now, the once thriving city is in ruins. It can no longer be rebuilt. It can only be torn down and built again from scratch. Tourists now gawk through the fence at the ruins. In just over forty years, the entire city, left to itself, decayed. Not from bombs. Just from being left alone.

Things left to themselves naturally decay. Just leave your yard alone for a month, or your car for a year, or your marriage for....

Jedaiah's own sons had now grown up playing on Jerusalem's fallen rocks. He had always believed that that one day the leaders would start rebuilding the walls. Everyone around him was negative, but during his teens, some of his friends thought it could be done. They had talked and talked about it. But nothing ever happened. Now, his sons use the nearby section of fallen rocks as a meeting place and neighborhood hangout. Jedaiah noticed none of those boys ever seemed to talk about it. Generations were slipping by with less and less apparent concern. They sat on the very stones that if someone just picked them up could be made into a wall or house.

To Jedaiah, the broken walls became a daily irritation, a daily reminder of his ineffectiveness. The walls that should have contained his dreams became the source of his despair. He became disappointed in those around him. Disappointed in circumstances, disappointed in God.

He knew the Scriptures and the psalms of David. He knew very well the Lord was their Shepherd, that God would protect them, that He would always cover them. Yet somewhere in the hopelessness of what he saw every day, Jedaiah lost the vision that David had written: "Though I walk through the valley of the shadow of death, my God will be with me."[2] Instead of the shadow of death, Jedaiah had embraced an actual death—the death of a dream.

We all walk through valleys in our lives. But, going up the other side of the valley is the only way to get to the tops of the mountains. Those valleys are not a place to camp. We don't stay in the shadow of the valley. We walk *through* the valley.

Unless it's dealt with, the shadow of disappointment will follow us, blocking us from the light of God's presence. I know men who have moved to different cities, changed jobs, even changed spouses trying to get away from the shadows…but the shadows follow. Shadows take the color out of your dreams.

SHADOWS TAKE THE COLOR OUT OF YOUR DREAMS.

Jesus told his friends on a regular basis, "Don't be dismayed. Don't be afraid. Don't be anxious. I am here. And my peace will be with you. My power will sustain you. Be full of hope."[3] Routinely, Jesus taught his followers about hope and about not falling victim to the negativity of the culture or the people around them.

Nehemiah arrived and heard the hopelessness in the local men. He was distraught. After all those years, after all those bands of people who said they were going to do something, he had expected to hear that someone had been working on at least part of the wall. In his disappointment, Nehemiah leaned into God. Hope began to pierce through the shadows.

Within days, Nehemiah's broken spirit would give birth to rebuilding broken walls.

Nehemiah announced they were going to rebuild the walls. He had letters of authority in his hand and an army behind him. The people marveled at his audacity. Some got excited. Hope began to dispel the darkened spiritual atmosphere. Jedaiah heard the good news, got past his fear, and just started.

Jedaiah was ready to work. He had just needed someone with vision to help him recover his heart and overcome the disappointment. His dream became vibrant once more. The hopes of his youth came alive.

He went home, gathered his sons and their friends, and started on that broken stretch of wall directly in front of his house. The playground, the hangout, his wife's clothesline—it was all coming down *and the wall was going up.*

Jesus came as Hope. Hope always defeats disappointment.

Broken people live next to broken walls. The broken walls are symbolic of shattered dreams and broken hearts.

Paul wrote this to the Romans about overcoming disappointment:

> *We can rejoice, too, when we run into problems and trials, for we know that they help us develop endurance. And endurance develops strength of character, and character strengthens our confident hope of salvation. And this hope will not lead to disappointment. For we know how dearly God loves us, because he has given us the Holy Spirit to fill our hearts with his love.*[4]

Walk out of the shadows. Hope has arrived.

Hope's name is Jesus.

14

DISTRACTION

The classic American author John Steinbeck, looking back on a period of declining creativity, wrote, "True things gradually disappeared and shiny easy things took their place."[1]

Something shinier, newer, more attractive, easier always flies by. We are easily distracted.

At dinner with friends one evening, one of the men said, "My new project would be tremendous, but I just keep getting off track. I think I'm just severely ADD."

Not to diminish those who have been diagnosed, it does seem the entire world has gone ADD. It's become a catchword for those who are easily distracted, which seems like almost everyone. I certainly feel that way at times.

A few minutes later at that same dinner someone was telling a story and the same man who had complained of getting off track absentmindedly said, "Wait, I was distracted, what did you say?" We all laughed.

Distraction is the enemy's hammer.

I had a close friend who was a captivating speaker, the pastor of an influential church, a man's man, and a friend's friend. He always had a quick word of encouragement at just the right time. As he was becoming well-known across the nation, and then around the world, we spent time together—dinners with our wives, trips together as couples. We always fell into fascinating and meaningful conversations. He loved what he was doing and he loved people. And then...it all crashed.

He got distracted. It wasn't fame or accolades. It wasn't extramarital affairs or mismanagement of finances. It was love of money. He became enamored with what he could purchase. It overwhelmed him. His dream as a young business owner had been to become very wealthy. Then he committed his life to Christ and began to invest his time in ministering to others. His pastor discovered he was a natural preacher and helped him hone his speaking skills. Soon my friend set out to be a full-time pastor, taking his wife and children with him. It was a huge step of faith, but they were extremely successful.

In all that time, he never resolved his youthful desire for the world's riches. He could not settle for the true wealth of godly pursuits.[2] He wanted money and he wanted what money could buy right here, right now. The old dream came back to life.

Late on Sunday nights he'd watch *Lifestyles of the Rich and Famous.* He justified it, saying it helped him decompress after a day of ministry. He drank in the opulent images and greed filtered into his life—a huge distraction that opened his heart to other excesses. The result was a slow decay of his character, his church, his closest friendships, and eventually his marriage. Distraction produced death.

On June 5, 1976, the 305-feet-high Teton Dam in Idaho had just been completed, and the massive lake was being filled with water. What the engineers didn't see was that the $100 million structure had been weakened by small cracks in the substructure. The foundation was compromised and small leaks had appeared. They didn't look to be a problem, until the dam collapsed—releasing 80 billion gallons of water that swept down the canyon and crushed over 300 square miles of land and cities. Eleven people died.

Small leaks, small distractions. They don't look like much...but they can collapse your dreams.

━━━━━━━━

Nehemiah went to Jerusalem with a hard enough battle on his hands—rebuilding the walls. Then, in the middle of the fight, the enemy tried every temptation and strategy to distract him.

The leaders in that region did not want a strong Jerusalem. They knew they were stronger and had more power over the people when Jerusalem was broken. So they sent letters to Nehemiah. They made accusations, threatened war, derided the local workers, heaped scorn on Nehemiah and his leaders.

THE MORE DISTINCTLY WE SEE OUR PURPOSE, THE MORE IT'S WORTH FIGHTING FOR.

Years later, people would say many things about Jesus. He ignored them, or He taught them... but He was never thrown off course by them. He was not distracted.

Nehemiah had to resist distraction. It was a massive battle.

The Bible teaches us to resist the attacks of the enemy. We might think the enemy is going to inflict us with massive barriers of illness or major financial issues or stress. But small distractions are far more common. Distractions have destroyed the most powerful of men.

How do we resist distraction? Our first, most important fight is in our own hearts. We have to resolve the purpose of our lives, and discard what doesn't fit. We access the power of God's presence to build clarity. The more distinctly we see our purpose, the more it's worth fighting for. Remember, *victory is always on the other side of a fight.*

We resist distraction by looking ahead, pressing forward, working hard. We resist distraction by focusing our hearts on our purpose. We resist distraction by having a firm resolve.

This is who I am.

This is what I'm about.

I will not be denied.

Every person is hit with distractions. Even good things can be distracting when they're outside of our purpose. We must be ready to fight distraction our whole lives.

What marks a man who achieves his dreams is the quiet resolve to keep moving toward them. To discard the distractions of negative talk, of defeats and wounds, of mistakes and temptations. To walk through the valleys.

The disciples were constantly distracted, but they fought to keep on track. To be a *disciple* means to practice *discipline*. That's the essence of a disciple—not one who is perfect, but a man who will discipline his life, who will fight for it. An athlete does not discipline himself because he hates himself, but because he wants to win. Discipline defeats distraction.

Fight the small distractions. Discipline and win.

15

TEMPTATION

"The essence of temptation is—it's tempting." Even in translation, that got a laugh from a group of men I was speaking to in Brazil. It's true everywhere, all over the world. Temptation is tempting.

Think about it. When you were not following Christ, you didn't really deal with temptation. In fact, before you were a Christian you probably didn't call it "temptation." You called it "opportunity."

The Bible tells us that every man is tempted. Even Jesus was tempted. Here's the issue most of us face as Christian men: we equate temptation with sin. We make temptation equal to messing up. But temptation isn't sin—temptation is what produces sin.

If temptation were sin, then Jesus would have sinned. Jesus didn't sin.

The Bible says that Jesus was tempted. That means there was actually something He wanted, something His humanity desired.

Look at what Satan offered Jesus to tempt Him. Jesus had been fasting so He'd been hungry a long time. Satan offered bread, or at least a way to make bread. Questioning His identity and motives, Satan said, "Why not just make some of these stones into bread?" It was tempting. In His physical body, Jesus was hungry.

TEMPTATION ISN'T SIN— TEMPTATION IS WHAT PRODUCES SIN.

Immediately Jesus modeled for us all how to defeat temptation—with the Word of God. Jesus quoted Scripture. *"No! The Scriptures say, 'People do not live by bread alone, but by every word that comes from the mouth of God.'"*[1]

Jesus was speaking of you and me spiritually. Our bread, our food, is literally His Word. His Word sustains us, grows us, nourishes us, strengthens us.

David wrote, *"I have hidden your word in my heart, that I might not sin against you."*[2] He said in essence, "The only way I can overcome temptation is to have a strong foundation of the presence of God in my heart and life. His Word protects my heart."

Satan then gave Jesus two more temptations. One was to jump off a high tower to prove who He was. But Jesus was concrete in His identity. He didn't need to prove anything. When you know who you are, you don't have to prove it, you just live it. And that's the proof. Again, Jesus spoke the Word of God.

Then came the big one, a final temptation that Satan knew would work. It was his trick play. The enemy showed Jesus the kingdoms of the world and all the turmoil, degradation, and pain. He showed Jesus children being abused, men being betrayed, women being misused, and families being torn apart. This wasn't a series of vacation photos—castles and lakes and amusement parks. He showed Jesus everything happening to God's creation. This was gut-wrenching.

Satan said, "Hey, I'll give You the entire world if You'll just worship me." This may have been the heaviest of all temptations, to bypass the cross, and all that personal pain, and stop everyone else's pain. To a man with a heart full of love and compassion, this temptation was real.

But Jesus was fully committed. He said, "Satan, get out of here. The Word says you must worship the Lord your God, and serve only Him."[3] Satan split. Jesus won. The Word of God brought victory.

Every temptation of Christ was an attack on His identity. The series of attacks began with, "If you are the Christ." Satan is always attacking your identity because from your identity comes forth your decisions and your destiny. Every temptation is an attack to cause you to deny who you are as a man, to deny your values, and to deny Christ.

Temptation is tempting. It's a fight. Jesus had to fight. You do, too. But, the fact you were tempted does not mean you sinned. Do not accept the accusations of the enemy. Use the Word of God as a powerful weapon.

I was on a flight to Atlanta and noticed the man next to me seemed agitated, like something was wrong. I didn't want to talk, didn't feel like it—but I felt the Lord prompting me. I grabbed a cup of tepid airline coffee and launched in. It was the dullest opening to a conversation:

"So, where you headed?" He told me. Then quiet.

Ok, cool, maybe I'm off the hook. Take a sip of coffee, check my spirit. Nope.

"What do you do?" He told me. More quiet.

Come on! The Lord wouldn't let me go—kept nudging my heart.

"So, you like what you're doing? Feeling fulfilled?"

And, then it started coming out. Robert began to tell me his business struggles. After a while I said, "But, man, that doesn't sound all that bad. Seems tough but normal business stuff. Seems like something else is really pulling on your guts. What's that?"

A real risk, but I felt compelled to take it.

"Ah man, my wife just dropped me off at the plane for this trip, and as I was getting on, my girlfriend called me. She's wanting a lot of time with me when I get back. My wife's planned a party for our kids. It's a mess. I don't know why I'm telling you this."

"I do," I said. "I'm a specialist in this stuff."

Over the next hour, we talked, ending with a time of prayer. As we got off the plane, I walked with Robert over to the side. He called the girlfriend and told her he was out. It was over. Then he called his wife. Robert was getting it done. I stood watching him on his phone, knowing I'd never forget this moment. A stranger I had just met, but now a brother in Christ.

Robert had been in a war without the right weapons. Trying to win the battles in his own strength was impossible. After being defeated, feeling deflated, furious with himself and taking it out on others, he had now finally won.

We shared contact information, so I followed up with him a few weeks later. He was smiling. Life was good. He had just purchased a new company with some partners and his family was moving. His wife was overjoyed. He was free.

Temptation comes to every man. You must have the right weapons to fight, and then you have to fight. You must rise up to the challenge— even when you don't want to. That's why God sent His Spirit to be part of every man's life that is a follower of Jesus. We have a secret weapon. It's like being Tony Stark and putting on your Iron Man suit of armor. No longer the enemy's prey, you're now dangerous to the enemy. (Read about how to put on the armor of God in Ephesians chapter 6.)

At every turn, the enemy is trying to kill you. He comes as a thief and a destroyer. He wants to destroy your dreams, your family, your life, your future. "All sin promises to please and serve but only desires to enslave and dominate," my dad taught me. That woman who wants some time with you is an enemy plot. She might be a nice person, but she herself is caught up in a larger scheme. Get out of there! Run!

Temptation is not sin. It's what you do with it that can make it sin. Be on guard. Be alert. Get the Word in your heart and keep it alive.

I've seen many men succumb to temptation because they were tired. A stranger taught me something about that. On another flight, this time to Florida, I had a conversation with a mature woman as she headed to a four-day vacation in Miami. She told me her story.

Her husband had been a developer in Nevada. When he died, the people around her told her to sell the company. She was on the way to doing just that, and driving down the street to the meeting, when she knew in her heart she could run the company. If it was so valuable, she thought, she should just keep it. And she did. But the stress was new to her and almost overwhelmed her right from the start. So, she started a pattern to deal with the stress. Every month, she takes a four-day vacation. Sometimes with friends, sometimes alone. Sometimes near, sometimes far. For the two weeks after the short time away, she's refreshed as she works. For the next ten days, she's looking forward to her next getaway. I never forgot that.

A business mentor of mine years ago said, "I can do twelve months of work in eleven months, but I can't do twelve months of work in twelve months."

Judi and I have practiced this. Sometimes we grab just an overnight getaway or a few days to refresh. We also plan annual times of refreshing. Fishing is built into my schedule. It's not just a hobby. It's renewal. I also sit on my back porch a few mornings every time I'm home and spend time just reading. I get my spirit quiet, rest my soul, and build energy for the next push.

When the fights come, I'm rested, ready.

Do this. It doesn't have to be costly. Judi and I have had some very frugal getaways. We stay some place inexpensive, then sit on the deck of a nearby luxury resort and order a cheese plate. We gather in the ambience, the quiet, the beauty...but only pay for the cheese. (Our little secret—now yours.)

How heavy for Jesus was this time of fasting and temptation and wrestling with Satan? I think it was a tough fight, because the minute He got home from the battle, He moved to a different city. He left the land-locked dusty village of Nazareth for the lakeside retreat of Capernaum. The name "Capernaum" means "place of refreshing." Tough fight—wise follow-up.

You must fight. You have no choice. I wrote in my book *Daring* that you were born into a world at war. And since you've been in a fight, you need some rest. No professional fighter or sports team goes into the next match or game before they rest. They renew. You need that, too.

Fight. Rest. Renew. Fight again.

But here's one more reality that Robert learned when we met on that flight. If you fall into temptation, we have God's word that He will forgive us. A friend said it well, "When you mess up, repent, *and repent quick!*" You don't have to feel bad for a week, or two weeks, trying to justify God's grace or look good in God's eyes. God's not looking for some sort of religious payment or show of piety. Jesus already made the payment. So, repent, get up, and move on.

One of the biblical passages that gives me daily strength is Psalm 37:23–24. It says, "*The* Lord *directs the steps of the godly. He delights in every detail of their lives. Though they stumble, they will never fall, for the* Lord *holds them by the hand.*"[4]

God knows us. He knows our stuff. He didn't say, *if* we stumble, but *when* we stumble. We all mess up. And God is always there for us. He said: "*If we confess our sins to him, he is faithful and just to forgive us our sins and to cleanse us from all wickedness.*"[5]

Temptation comes to every man. We defeat temptation with the Word of God. If we stumble, we repent. He is a God who is faithful to forgive.

16

STRATEGY

When Nehemiah arrived, hope arrived. He had an army, he had the king's favor, he had some money, and he had a strategy. Strategy trumps passion.

Jedaiah and his sons put in long hours, encouraged by Nehemiah and the supplies he had. The whole neighborhood rallied to help. On one side, Rephaiah, the mayor of a section of the city, led crews to start building. Beside Rephaiah, the perfumer named Hananiah went out in the choking dust and heat to start building, which both surprised and encouraged his neighbors. On his other side, Jedaiah's longtime friend Hattush put his family and neighbors to work. Two sections past him, Shallum and his daughters were out working. Camaraderie grew as everyone worked toward one purpose and admired the job their friends were doing on either side. *The walls were going up!*

My friend Geoff Gorsuch wrote in his great book *Brothers!*, "Women bond face to face, but men bond shoulder to shoulder facing a challenge."[1] The people were becoming a force...by the power of one man's vision.

And then.....

Fifty-two days after they started, the people *finished*.

The walls had been broken for over ninety years. They were rebuilt in fifty-two days. It wasn't easy. It was a fight. There were many obstacles. But the impossible was possible for a community of willing workers with a shared vision.

Nehemiah added wisdom to his dream and created a strategy. From Solomon's proverbs, we learn the first thing God created was wisdom.[2] Wisdom is the architect of all creation. Wisdom gives us the ability to make the right decision based on full knowledge and understanding. We are to get wisdom before we get anything else. It is "...*the principal thing*."[3]

A wide gulf exists between the kinds of wisdom people have. Diamond smugglers are wise about their routes and avoiding being caught. Drug dealers display wisdom in building markets and manipulating people. That's all earthly wisdom. It's finite, based on human understanding. Godly wisdom has a righteous foundation and produces good, lasting results that benefit everyone.

But if you harbor bitter envy and selfish ambition in your hearts, do not boast about it or deny the truth. Such "wisdom" does not come down from heaven but is earthly, unspiritual, demonic.[4]

Now this is our boast: Our conscience testifies that we have conducted ourselves in the world, and especially in our relations with you, with integrity and godly sincerity. We have done so, relying not on worldly wisdom but on God's grace.[5]

What's interesting about earthly wisdom is that so often it looks right. We as men need to stop ourselves and say, "Wait, did I pray about this, is this really a good, godly idea?"

A friend took me to lunch and confided, "So much of what I do seems like I really know what I'm doing. But then you see companies—big ones—go bankrupt, great couples get divorced, nice people's kids get on drugs. Millions of cars every year are recalled for all kinds of issues. Let's not even start on the government...."

"Kyle, you're so successful, kicking it on every level." I didn't just say it because he bought my lunch. He really is.

"I know, I know. But it's really just James 1:5. If you need wisdom, ask our generous God, and He will give it to you. He will not rebuke you for asking. You just can't be afraid to ask."

"You know, you're right, guys are afraid they'll get rebuked." I started thinking about a young man I'd recently had coffee with who had made one bad decision after another.

"You know, compared to the executives I work with, I didn't grow up in the right family, or live in the right city, or go to the right school," Kyle said. "In a sense, I don't belong. And, it was hard for me to learn that God wasn't going to put me down just because I admitted I didn't have the right answer. But once I got past that, I gained an inexhaustible source of wisdom others just don't have. I'm known in my line of work for doing the right thing at the right time. That's what wisdom gives you."

Kyle constantly gives me great counsel and enlarges my heart. I asked, "A young man came to me asking for advice. He just seems incapable of making a good decision. Can I tell him your story?"

"Sure, man. Send him to me and I'll tell him if he won't listen to you. It's kind of obvious God knows more. God is not derisive toward us. The guy just has to *ask*."

I walked out to my car and looked up the word "derisive." Kyle, stretching me again. Then I headed to my next meeting with the aimless young man I was mentoring.

I had given him a Bible and pointed out Proverbs and Psalms to him. I encourage men to read Proverbs every morning, based on the day of the month—Proverbs 11 on the eleventh day of the month, and so on. And I encourage them to read Psalms at night to get courage.

My dad taught me that. Then, when I started into business as a young entrepreneur, Dad taught me that godly wisdom brings the right strategy and the right strategy brings victory. Depending on who you are, victory could mean a better bottom line, or harmony in your family, or some big win. Whatever the obstacle, wisdom brings the strategy to overcome the obstacle and achieve that victory.

Nehemiah's strategy worked so well, the task that people thought was impossible for one hundred years got done in less than two months. Part of the strategy was to let everyone work on their portion of the project in the way they could. Men good at mixing mortar did that, men good at busting rocks did that, and as they each worked using their gifts, the walls went up *fast*.

Agreement produces power. It was true for Nehemiah, it's true in your company, true in your church, true in your family. Agreement as parents produces harmony and authority in the home. Agreement as church leaders produces a powerful outreach. Wherever there is fundamental disagreement, wisdom is lost. Jesus himself taught that disagreement results in powerlessness, but agreement produces power.[6]

That day, I needed to help the young man learn to ask for wisdom like Kyle did, so he could get a strategy to reach his place of victory. And, he needed to come into agreement with his own dream. He was like so many guys. His heart wanted the dream. His mind just wanted to hang out. One of those would win.

We all want victory. But victory is always the result of the right strategy. My father taught me the pattern—Wisdom, Strategy, Victory.

Dwayne Pickett, Sr., is a wonderful friend and pastor who has packed a lot of life into a very few years. His grandfather was an entrepreneur. One of his holdings was a speakeasy in the country outside of Jackson, Mississippi. When Dwayne was just sixteen years old, he had his own bar tab where he could bring any of his friends. He would watch as one after another famed blues players came through. Some of the most famous blues artists in the world—and some of the most notorious gamblers. Gunfights were so common, Dwayne and his brother Charles would sit up in the woods when they were younger just to watch.

In that environment, Dwayne's life became hell-bound, enough that his dad, a university administrator, took out a life insurance policy on him when he was just fifteen years old. His dad knew he'd probably be dead by twenty-one and wanted to have the money for a good funeral.

After Dwayne accepted Jesus Christ as his Lord and Savior, he felt called to minister. It's a long story, but God knew the dreams placed in Dwayne's heart, even if Dwayne didn't acknowledge them yet. In his path to becoming a university professor, Dwayne was redirected by God and called to become a pastor.

Two years after becoming a follower of Christ, on March 5, 1992, Dwayne had written in his personal prayer journal: "I know that God has called me to minister to men. Particularly to young black men." Eventually, he became the senior pastor of New Jerusalem Missionary Baptist Church, a historic congregation in the city of Jackson. In 1963, the great civil rights pioneer Medgar Evers had spoken at the church hours before he was assassinated in his driveway a few blocks away.

Dwayne plowed into ministry with energy. He led his men on retreats, did men's breakfasts, tried all different ways of achieving his dream to minister to young men. It wasn't having lasting results. Then, in what seemed like a coincidence, Dwayne and I met in Indonesia. We connected immediately. He's like that. I introduced him to the Majoring in Men curriculum, a strategic, proven path for discipling men. Now, following the strategy God has given him, New Jerusalem Church is raising up hundreds of strong men, "commissioning" them to lead their families and communities, to accept responsibility and lead as Christ did, by giving their lives.

Last week, Dwayne and I drove out to the ruins of his grandfather's nightclub. Now it sits in the middle of hundreds of acres of land that will be used for camps for young men. He told me, "Paul, when I found the strategy to disciple men, it changed everything. Look—I had the passion, I just didn't have the pattern. Now we have multiple campuses and in all of our weekend services we have over 40 percent men in attendance. That's unheard of in our culture. And I know those men have my back. They're ready to get involved and they're eager to invest. It's remarkable."

We looked at the ruins of the speakeasy and what came to mind was the Scripture in Isaiah chapter 61 that declares, "I will bring beauty from ashes and will give joy where there has been discouragement."[7]

God gives us wisdom to develop a strategy. Ask for wisdom. Find the strategy, achieve victory.

17

FIGHT

I was in Nashville, speaking for my friend Wes at a morning meeting of business leaders who come together for encouragement and to plan community improvement works. Wes said later that the talk really hit him. What I told the men gathered that morning was this: your identity is what fights or gives up.

You will not fight for what you are not, or for what you deem is worthless. You will fight for what you hold as worthy of value.

Your identity is your most valuable asset.

Your identity is the definition of who you are. Nehemiah is a compelling hero because he refused to be defined by his position, by others' expectations, by his past, by his employment, or by his own flaws. He leveraged his position, his friendships, and everything he knew to follow God's call. When he did, he left security for significance. Risk precedes success.

Nehemiah was defined by his faith in God. And that's the fight. It's the world aligned against your identity because you're aligned with Christ.

YOUR IDENTITY IS WHAT FIGHTS OR GIVES UP.

Remember, the world defines a man by what he does with his hands. God defines a man by who he is in his heart. A man's dreams start in his heart, empowered by his identity. What is in his heart, we later see through his hands. First your heart, then your hands.

When you find your identity in Christ, and embrace the new dreams in your heart, God will put into your hands the tools to fulfill what is in your heart.

First the heart, then the hands.

First the character, then the talent.

First new life, then new decisions.

GOD WILL PUT INTO YOUR HANDS THE TOOLS TO FULFILL WHAT IS IN YOUR HEART.

If a man's dreams are counter to his identity, he lives in disagreement with himself, disharmony. A conflicted man will wander in a complicated cloud of confusion. A man who knows his identity becomes clear in his decisions, strong in his faith, and energized in his work.

Paul wrote to men in Rome, "Let God transform you into a new person, by changing the way you think."[1]

Your heart is the foundational source of your thoughts. Your thoughts shape your identity. Your identity forms your decisions. Your decisions create your destiny.

Here is the pattern that rolls out of identity: identification, involvement, investment, increase.

When a man is identified with Christ by salvation, he gets involved. Reading his Bible, meeting at church, praying for others. Then he begins to invest. He invests his time, his skills, his money. From that investment comes increase to him, and to others. A man's life increases as he follows Christ, in that his life becomes larger.

Friendships are deeper. Dreams steer toward helping others more than self. It happens subtly. When we turn our hearts to Christ, we are imbued with His DNA—and He is always about helping others.

———

Nehemiah arrived in Jerusalem after a grueling journey. But the obstacles he faced there were larger than anything he had ever encountered. Local armies threatened to kill the entire population, to destroy their homes and tear down the part of the wall they had built so far. To solve it, Nehemiah armed the workers. He wrote, "So we held a hammer in one hand and a sword in the other."[2]

They were not expecting it to be easy, but they were not going to be intimidated into stopping the work. They had a shared vision.

When the king of Persia gave Nehemiah all he needed for the journey and the work of rebuilding, the Bible says that Nehemiah found favor with the king.[3] He had favor with the king, but now he had to fight.

Favor always attracts a fight.

+ Gideon had the favor of God and ended up in multiple wars.
+ Joseph had favor and ended up in prison.
+ Moses had favor and ended up running for his life, going up against the Red Sea and other obstacles until he died.
+ Abraham had favor and went through betrayals and disappointments.
+ Jesus' disciples had favor and ten of them were martyred.
+ Mary had favor and found herself unmarried and pregnant.

Every one of those champions was doing what God wanted. When Moses arrived at the Red Sea and was surrounded by a king's army behind him, mountains on both sides, and the ocean in front of him, it was not because he had missed hearing God or he had a bad map. It was because God was going to prove His power. When Moses was faithful, he ended up in a fight.

Most of the addiction issues that men deal with today are really a way of dealing with a poor personal definition. Why do men turn away from the God who wants to renew and restore their lives? Because they have defined God wrongly. They have let others define who God is. And, most men have let others define who *they* are.

———

One compelling moment in Jerusalem shows us the complete change in self-awareness that Nehemiah had. He had learned who he was, why he was there, and how big his God was.

The walls were being built. Nehemiah, his brother, and others were directing the construction—a slave, and a bunch of men who had lived in oppression their whole lives. Some messengers arrived from the regional kings. *Kings!* This was Nehemiah's world. He knew their power, knew their message demanded an answer. The message was that the kings wanted to meet with Nehemiah.

The first time the invitations came, the messages were cordial. Nehemiah was intensely focused. He threw them on the ground at the feet of the messengers' horses and kept building.

The messengers arrived again. This time the letters contained threats of destruction. Nehemiah tossed them aside again. But this time he sent out orders to arm all the workers. He would not be intimidated. *Let's get some weapons.*

After the threat of war, Nehemiah gathered all his captains, leaders, and governors and made one of the greatest declarations ever uttered:

"Don't be afraid of the enemy! Remember the Lord, who is great and glorious, and fight for your brothers, your sons, your daughters, your wives, and your homes!"[4]

Then he instructed them to rush to the fight.

"When you hear the blast of the trumpet, rush to wherever it is sounding. Then our God will fight for us!"[5]

———

The Battle of Yarmouk took place in August of AD 636 and it fundamentally changed the world we live in. The forces of Islam came against the armies of the Byzantine Empire and its Western allies in the northern areas of modern-day Iraq. The allied forces were marked by infighting, mismanaged supply lines, and poor preparation. The result was the first major victory for Islam.

That defeat of the West over 1,400 years ago is still the center point for massive issues in Iraq and the Middle East. It has spilled across every part of the globe and is affecting our lives every day.

The issue was that the Western allies and the Byzantine forces didn't have a compelling vision. Their identity was personal, selfish, and narrow. They fought over little things, bickered, squabbled among themselves. The Islamic forces were united, they were passionate, they were skillful. The Western guys were arrogant.

When it's time to fight, it's time to get focused and just *fight*.

Without a compelling identity and vision, we can all get selfish and narrow real quick.

At an extremely difficult period of time in my life, I wrote this to myself. I recently found it in the back of an old journal.

It holds deep meaning to me, so I share it as a friend:

Fight.

Fight in the sneering face of evil…
   fight in the crunching grip of temptation…
   fight in the free-falling depths of darkness…
   fight and don't stop fighting.

Fight when you have fallen…fight when you can't move…
   fight when it seems desperately hopeless…
   fight and don't stop fighting.

Fight when you feel no imminent victory…
   fight when the path is slippery and treacherous…
   fight in the valley of indecision…
   fight and don't stop fighting.

Fight when others have turned back...fight through the lingering guilt...
 fight while crawling to the breach of light...
 fight and don't stop fighting.

Fight though you have no breath...fight in the searing despair of pain...
 fight in the blood, sweat, and vomit...
 fight with the desperation of drowning...

Fight and don't stop fighting...

Victory only comes to the enduring fighter.

18

LEGACY

At the feet of Nehemiah the ruins of history lay in the broken rocks. But he was about to put into motion something more powerful than bricks and mortar. It was a legacy of faith.

One day, a message came from the neighboring kings. Nehemiah received message after message from neighboring kings with threats for him to quit. The fifth message was a carefully worded accusation that Nehemiah was doing all this so he could make himself the king of Jerusalem. The kings implored him to come meet with them and explain himself.

Nehemiah squarely stood himself on the word that God had given him, the faith he had in his heart, the trust others had shown in him. He said, "Should a man like me be intimidated by them? Should I come down and meet them, and defend myself? I will not!"[1]

I never get tired of reading his declaration: "A man like me." Something had changed in his heart. A huge shift had taken place. Nehemiah was still a slave, but now he was a fully committed man with the strength of godly vision, identity, and purpose. He was the same man, but he was a different person. He knew all about kings, how they viewed themselves, and the absolute rule they lorded over their people. He told those kings to take a hike.

WHAT A MAN DOES IN LIFE BECOMES HISTORY. WHAT HE PUTS INTO MOTION BECOMES LEGACY.

Nehemiah's identity became his greatest strength. His identity protected his heart, it protected his family, and it protected the people around him. Who you are is not just about you. It's always going to be about others. Every decision you make affects people around you and people who are coming after you in life.

Identity is built on the foundation of acceptance. When a father accepts his son, it becomes foundational to a healthy identity. Whether he had a father or not, when a man finds his acceptance in God, it becomes the foundation of his identity. God accepts us. He sent His Son to prove His love, and to reconnect us. Forgiveness proved acceptance. When the king embraced Nehemiah's dreams, accepted that he was the man who could accomplish the task, it built Nehemiah's confidence, faith, and inner security.

Nehemiah's identity helped the nation rediscover its national identity. The nation's identity had been buried in rubble. As workers raised the wall, the people regained the bold identity that had once beaten strong in their hearts and reigned in their streets. A new era began.

Your identity energizes your dreams.

What a man does in life becomes history.

What he puts into motion becomes legacy.

So many men tell me, "Who am I to do anything...what could I ever do?" They need an identity infusion.

Consider the life of an unknown little woman named Ethel Dean.

In July 1991, at the age of ninety-eight, a lady in a small, nondescript house in Los Angeles passed away. Just eighteen relatives and friends attended her funeral. Living alone for over fifty years, many would say that Ethel Dean lived and died without much impact in the world.

But Ethel Dean had three sisters—Mabel, Berta, and Florence. At the age of twenty-four, Ethel had met Jesus Christ as her Lord and Savior. Day after day, she would write letters of hope and grace to her sisters.

In tear-stained letter after letter she shared the love of her heavenly Father, the forgiveness of Christ, and the power of the Holy Spirit. After months of letters, one sister, then another, then the last accepted Jesus Christ as Lord and Savior.

One sister, Florence, was so taken by her newfound relationship with God that she immediately enrolled in a Bible college in Los Angeles. Weekend nights would find Florence on the street corners of LA, preaching the gospel—dragging her twelve-year-old son along reluctantly to play the trombone. That young man, with an unsaved father, went through tough times of indecision, but Florence and her sister Ethel wouldn't let go of him in faith. During World War II, as the kamikaze attacks came on his ship in the Pacific naval battles, they prayed, and miraculously the diving bombers missed his ship.

Following the war, the extraordinary day came when Florence found out her son was attending a Sunday night church service with his boss, Ralph Calkins. Florence called Ethel, told her to pray, then drove to the city where he lived, parked down the street, got in the back seat of her car, and prayed all afternoon. That night her son committed his life to Christ and was called into the ministry.

Thirty years later, that man sat in a small hotel room in Pittsburgh, Pennsylvania, and in a five-day blitz wrote a book called *Maximized Manhood*.

The son of Ethel Dean's sister Florence was named Edwin. My dad.

> The legacy of that soft-spoken, unseen little lady named Ethel Dean is a powerful global ministry that touches the lives of millions of people.
>
> Ethel Dean never got any credit. She lived ninety-eight years somewhat anonymously, but her precious, handwritten, tear-stained letters carried the weight of eternity for millions of people.

Unexpected people change the world.

If you've read this far, maybe you've heard me say this before:

Go!

Start!

Jesus didn't come to change the world—He came to save the world. The world changed because Jesus came. Help people and the world will change. The world changes for you, and for the person you helped, for the person you loved—and maybe for a lot more people after that.

Go help someone—call them—write them a note—minister life—love deeply—and, change the world. I believe in you. And so does God.

19

CAPACITY

Bill and I were fishing a small, remote Alaskan river in a four-man inflatable. It was a crisp, cool day with fast-moving, ice-cold water. Skies were blue with a few trailing, ultra-white clouds. An occasional hawk took a look at us. We had hot coffee in the thermos, trout on the line. Quite a day.

We sometimes broke our silence to talk about family, sports, or business. Bill had started a couple of businesses that had done well, and a couple not-so-great ones. Now he had pushed through difficult times and was highly successful.

"I guess I just got to where I could handle stuff," he said. "I got larger through it all. The stuff that upset or stressed me in my early days wasn't as stressful after a while. I persevered through the challenges. I learned to focus on the real issues and not get sidetracked."

"So, you got larger as a man," I said. He nodded. We fished.

Larger. Capacity. It's impossible to become highly successful without becoming a stronger, larger, more resilient person.

―――――――

Nehemiah began his journey to Jerusalem as the same man who had been a slave. Something had happened in his heart, but now

GOD GIVES US CAPACITY BECAUSE WE ARE NOT LARGE ENOUGH TODAY TO FIGHT TOMORROW'S BATTLES.

something started happening in his identity and his capacity. He began to see himself larger, more capable, stronger. He had a sense that he could accomplish his goals. Every step, every action stretched him.

Solomon was a great king who as a young man took over for his father David. He inherited a kingdom surrounded by enemies, filled with palace intrigue and the daily issues of a complex culture. He was up against some huge obstacles.

Solomon prayed. He asked for wisdom. Smart move. God responded by saying in essence, "You have asked for the right thing. Wisdom." God gave him wisdom but He also gave Solomon something he didn't ask for—something Solomon didn't even know to ask for, but God knew that he needed it. Like the king knew Nehemiah needed an army, God knew that Solomon needed one other element for success.

God gave Solomon wisdom, understanding, and *largeness of heart.* Largeness. Capacity.

God gives us capacity because we are not large enough today to fight tomorrow's battles. God essentially told Solomon, "I'll give you wisdom, but you're not large enough to contain the wisdom that I know you need. So, I'm going to increase the capacity of your heart and soul."

Capacity. Largeness of heart. It always comes by being stretched. Our heart directs our life, so if your life is to be larger, your heart must be larger. Your capacity for wisdom, pain, stress, turmoil, compassion, generosity, love—it must all get larger. We get stretched.

You will only rise to the level of leadership for which you are willing to accept the pain. And, you are only qualified to lead to the degree you are willing to serve. That takes a large heart and the willingness to endure the pain of humility, anonymity, or correction. The greater a man's humility, the larger the man.

The Marines say, "Pain is weakness leaving my body."

Most men want the position without the pain. Being stretched involves pain…sometimes a great deal of pain. The level of pain is directly related to the level of position a man desires. A small man put into a large position will shrink the position to match the capacity of his heart, which has shrunk to his pain threshold. The payment for position is pain. It is the currency of greatness.

Most men are not fighting for their identity. They're not even looking. They're waiting for someone else to tell them what their identity is. There's no pain involved in that. No stretching.

Getting stretched is how capacity happens. Bill had experienced huge stretching moments. He endured the pain of those times he thought he would never get through, obstacles that looked too large, problems that looked impossible, and all of it stretched him.

There are two ways you can stretch to build capacity: intimacy and adversity.

Our most important stretching place is intimacy with the Father—practicing His presence, prayer, Word, time with the "brethren," worship, meditation on the Word, fasting, the spiritual disciplines.

The height of a building is directly related to the depth of the foundation. Build a strong foundation, you'll build a durable and robust life. Your heart is your foundation. It is what's in your heart that will sustain you through the journey of life. When your heart is larger, you can build a larger life. Intimacy with God expands your heart and deepens your life.

Jesus said, "*I have told you all this so that you may have peace in me. Here on earth you will have many trials and sorrows. But take heart, because I have overcome the world.*"[1] Paul said to the people in Rome, "*Rejoice in our confident hope. Be patient in trouble, and keep on praying.*"[2] Intimacy with God produces faith. Strength. Confidence.

Deeper love. Hope. Hope is the complete confidence that God will keep His word. Intimacy with God stretches you.

We increase capacity by intimacy, and also by adversity. Jesus said we would have adversity. His half-brother James experienced trouble. James saw his brother crucified. James was persecuted. James knew the sting of betrayal.

James wrote, *"When troubles of any kind come your way, consider it an opportunity for great joy.... When your faith is tested, your endurance has a chance to grow. So let it grow, for when your endurance is fully developed, you will be perfect and complete, needing nothing."*[3] James basically said, "Obstacles make you larger." He knew the result of facing adversity was increased strength, largeness of heart, and greater capacity in the inner man.

What stops you? Little voices of doubt? Nagging defeat from the past? Inferiority? Comments from negative people? Facing those trials in Christ will strengthen your heart, and make you a larger man. An old prophet named Zechariah said our victories come this way: "It's not by your strength or your power, it's by the power of God."[4]

Building capacity through intimacy with God and by having His presence in adversity makes us more confident. One of the most powerful and needed attributes of a leader is confidence—being able to say, "Follow me, it's this way."

Men follow confident men. We don't follow wimps.

When we are confident, we are willing to take on greater challenges.

For many years I was the owner of a diverse marketing and media company. We had started small, did a few successful projects, and then became larger. In the 1980s, we experienced some big wins with some major projects. Then we got a call from a friend, and helped with the successful launch of FarmAid. We were feeling confident. The next year, we received a call from Paramount Pictures. They had a small movie that had done well in Australia, but had not started well in its initial rollout in the US. They were concerned. They contacted us.

We rolled out the movie in the top fifty markets combining rock stations, television outlets, Taco Bell stores, the Australia tourism commission, and other partners in a major push we pulled together in just a few weeks. My vice-president James, my lead strategist (and sister) Joann, and our team were feeling confident that we could tackle something big because we had pushed through some previous wins. The pain and stretching of smaller projects gave us the capacity for larger work.

That little movie, *Crocodile Dundee*, became a global phenomenon. Paramount was elated. We were successful. We never would have tackled that larger project unless we had built the confidence in the smaller projects. The pain of stretching in the smaller moments built the capacity for greater works.

Don't resist getting larger. Capacity starts in the private moments of intimacy with God, and is revealed in the public moments of adversity.

David was a young man chosen by God to be the next king of Israel after the disastrous reign of King Saul. Samuel was Israel's prophet called by God to find the next king and anoint him. After looking throughout the nation, God directed Samuel to an obscure but successful shepherd named Jesse who had eight sons. David was the youngest.

When Samuel showed up, Jesse brought out the oldest seven sons, thinking that one of them would be the next king. He didn't bring David to the lineup because the last person Jesse thought would be king was David. Samuel passed over all seven. He said, "You don't have any other sons?" Jesse dismissed it with, "Well, there's David." David was about thirteen years old when Samuel called him out and anointed him to be the next king.

After the anointing and celebration dinner, Jesse still thought so little of David that he sent him back out with the servants and hired hands. David's father did not affirm him. But out in the fields with the servants and sheep, in the quiet moments, in the places of intimacy and adversity, David grew large. He wrote songs, prayed, worked the sheep, and killed dangerous animals like lions and bears. His identity was forged in private, and would soon be revealed in public.

A few years after his anointing, David's brothers went off to war. For forty days and nights the armies of Israel and Philistia faced off in a massive valley. Tens of thousands of warriors were engaged. The Philistines sent out their toughest warrior, their champion, to challenge Israel to a "winner take all" duel. Goliath was a massive man of brute strength and must have been a nasty fighter. Just the fierceness of his voice caused men to cower. Every morning and evening for forty days, Goliath showed up at the center of the valley and screamed curses at Israel's army. "Where is your champion!" he would shout. The problem was, not one man in Israel thought of himself as a champion, so not one man responded.

Goliath is a picture of every obstacle we face as men. Every man faces Goliaths of temptations, trials, issues, betrayals, inferiorities, and disappointments. David, now about sixteen years old, had been sent by his dad to take food to his brothers on the front lines. His dad didn't send David to help fight, just to carry some biscuits.

When David arrived and Goliath called out for a champion, David's heart resonated. "That's me!" His brothers laughed at him, but God had given him a new identity. David was no longer the boy marginalized by his dad, or scoffed at by his brothers. He was a champion on the inside, and it was about to come out.

The private moments David spent with God gave him confidence in the public adversity of Goliath.

Hearing the call for a champion, David finally told the men around him, "That's me!"[5]

Most men today don't have an earthly father who has affirmed them. You may never have heard your dad say, "Nice one," or "You're awesome," or "You can do it." But like David, you can spend time with your Father in heaven and He will fill you with His love, affirmation, and faith. You are who God says you are.

Romans says, you are "more than a conqueror."[6] Bigger. Larger. Stronger than you believe you are, or anyone has ever told you. Finding your identity in Christ will always make you a more authentic and powerful man. You are a champion.

When David ran toward Goliath, he ran toward his identity. He killed Goliath. He had become a champion already on the inside. Defeating Goliath made it evident.

When Jesus began His ministry at the age of thirty, He launched it with a bold statement of His identity. He read from the scrolls in Isaiah chapter 61.

> The Spirit of the LORD is upon me, for he has anointed me to bring Good News to the poor. He has sent me to proclaim that captives will be released, that the blind will see, that the oppressed will be set free, and that the time of the LORD's favor has come.[7]

Because of Jesus' identity, we find our identity. In Christ, we become larger. When you kill the lions and bears in private, you can defeat the Goliaths in public. Embrace the pain, get larger. Larger capacity, greater success.

20

SEASON

Nehemiah was careful about dates and seasons in his memoir. He arrived in Jerusalem in the spring. But the season that changed most dramatically was a spiritual season.

When Nehemiah arrived, the nation's season changed from despair to hope, from dark to light, from defeat to triumph. In the new season, the people began to have a heart to work. Four hundred and fifty years later, when Jesus came, the season changed again....

Jesus arrived on the earth and hope arrived. In the midst of chaos, peace arrived. Jesus walked through the gates Nehemiah had built. He came as the Light of the World, as the Word of God...and that word was *redemption*. Three days after he hung on a cross, the season changed forever for mankind. A season of new life, a fresh spring in the destiny of the earth.

Seasons change. *We can't change the season, we can only adapt to the season.* We embrace its unique characteristics. Many have noted the phrase often used in Scripture, "And it came to pass." Thank God, the seasons don't come to stay.

The circadian rhythm of the ocean echoes the heartbeat of God, and the changing of the seasons echo the journeys of man. From transition to transition. All of life is a process of leaving one to enter another. How we leave the passing season will determine how we enter the next.

We tend to define ourselves moment to moment, and so we miss God's rhythms. There is a rhythm to what God creates. Scientists have found waves of electrons in the atmosphere that pulse with regularity. The ocean moves. Tides shift. People who love the desert will show you that it is teeming with seasonal life.

All of creation is built around the rhythm of seasons. Even places we think don't have seasons—like equatorial islands—have certain times it rains, certain times crops will be full, certain times the winds move into a season of doldrums and you cannot sail, seasons for rest, and seasons for reproduction.

What we have to learn is to weather the seasons in preparation for the season to change.

In a gripping scene from the documentary *The Bridge*, a man who tried to commit suicide by jumping off the Golden Gate Bridge talked about his attempt to kill himself. He was one of the few ever to survive.

As he and the filmmaker viewed actual footage of his jump, he commented that the moment he jumped, he knew he had made a terrible mistake. "The millisecond my hands left the rail, it was an instant regret."[1]

A bad day doesn't mean you're having a bad life. Don't make decisions based on the current season. Keep walking through it and the season will change. "This too shall pass."

Judi and I were having lunch with a young couple in La Jolla, California—incidentally, the city of my birth (no historic marker... yet). On a beautiful sunny afternoon, on the upstairs porch at Georges at the Cove, we sat and talked, enjoying our friendship.

The husband was hugely successful and full of energy. As he told us of his plan to expand their business, to take it to another level, you could see his wife's impatience grow. Judi and I love visionaries. We get pumped just being around people like that. We were caught up in his excitement, but noticed her reservation.

Finally his wife said, "I'm just concerned."

"About what?" Judi asked.

"His life is so full now, and this new journey will put him on the road night after night," his wife said.

"Well, that is a real concern, given that you have three children," Judi said. Judi had already lived through that when our children were small.

"So how long does this first season last?" I asked him.

"Based on experience, it will last three to four months," he said. "Very intense. I'll be gone most of the time. Raising capital, building the national staff, making it happen."

That got me thinking back to young Brent, the high school football coach. *"What pain could you not withstand if you knew that on the other side was your dream?"*

On the way back to our hotel, Judi and I talked about how many times I've had this conversation with men. It's not wise to create a lifestyle that is unbalanced. But…if it's just for a season, that doesn't mean it's an unbalanced lifestyle.

In one sense, the "balanced life" is a myth. Pedaling a bicycle seems normal, but only once you know how to ride one, and only once the bike is in motion. Getting it started is something else. Clinging to a balanced life instead of achieving your dreams is like walking a bike at an even pace year after year when you could have put it into motion, jumped on it, and one day been riding full speed down the slopes at Angel Fire or through the trails of Ogden, Utah.

Sometimes seasons arrive on top of you. You cannot change the season, you adapt to it. You stay faithful in it. You lean into God's Word.

Our friend Ryan and his family have a beautiful farm in Lancaster County, Pennsylvania. I've learned a lot about farming just listening to his passion for it. He's explained that he will only get a great harvest if he is faithful in the winter. A good farmer knows that the wintertime is as important as the harvest time. It's in the winter that you work on the equipment and the fields, and get prepared.

YOU CANNOT CHANGE THE SEASON, YOU ADAPT TO IT.

If Ryan was not faithful in the winter, there would be no harvest.

Seasons of intensity come and go.

To lay everything on the table, in hopes of achieving a dream, takes guts and then endurance. You pay the price of pain in order to experience the joy of success.

Years ago a special friend of mine was selling advertising packages to mid-sized businesses that wanted to sell their company. He would fly out most Monday mornings and fly back on Friday nights. Sometimes he'd get back on Thursday night if he had a good week. It was an intense season.

One wintry day he landed in Chicago, got a rental car, stopped at the first convenience store he saw and bought a roll of quarters. As the wind swept around him and the snow fell, he stood in a telephone booth plugging in quarters and going through the local telephone book to set up appointments.

His last quarter spent, and his page scribbled with the names of companies he had made appointments to visit the next day, he turned to leave the booth but found he couldn't move. He pulled hard on one leg until the ice below him cracked as one shoe loosed itself. Then he cracked loose the other one. His feet had frozen to the ground.

He called home that night to see how the children were, and to tell his wife about his calls and efforts. He told me recently that every day, month after month, year after year, as he called home, his wife would say, "I love you. I believe in you. We'll be here when you get home. I'm with you whatever it takes."

We have to be willing to pay the price. So simple. So hard.

The same friend, still making his living working in sales, was confident that if he would push through that season of his career, he would be successful. His wife continued to join in agreement with him, prayed for him, raised their children, encouraged him. He stayed after it year after year.

Then one day the owner of the company sat him down and asked, "Do you want to be a vice president?" It was a new season. Brian became an executive. Soon, he partnered with other executives and bought out that owner. Next, he bought out his partners. Today, he has built one of the largest brokerage firms in the nation.

The pain of freezing to the pavement was a season. He didn't just survive. He was faithful in the season, and now he's enjoying the success. He raised amazing children and enjoys a wonderful marriage. In agreement with his wife, the family paid the price most are unwilling to pay.

If he had not been faithful in the winter, he would have missed the harvest.

———————

We checked back with our friends from La Jolla months later. Our counsel to them was to be faithful in the difficult season, endure the discomfort, stay in agreement, pray together, work hard, trust God for the results. They were doing it. It wasn't easy. They had to revise some of their plans. But because they didn't try to change the season, they were becoming very fulfilled.

I hear this story constantly. The myth of the balanced life does not take into account the seasons of life. Staying at a drab job year after year to be balanced isn't always the best path. Would it be better for your children to have a role model who has aspirations, who is a lifelong learner, a man who stretches and grows throughout his life? Look at the long arch—face it truthfully, in reality. This is what it will take. And then measure the reward on the other side. Risk/reward. Seedtime/harvest. Winter/spring. Seasons.

Nehemiah knew the nation was in a season of intense work. He didn't hide the truth. He told the people they would have to work harder than they had ever worked—women and children included. Everyone would have to sacrifice, sweat, work, and endure.

Then the season changed—fifty-two days later, the walls were *up*. The first season of rebuilding was over. It wasn't easy. There were many obstacles. But living in the season had produced great success.

Storms come to every life. Even Jesus went through storms. Seasons change, winds blow. We enjoy the harvest times but tend to be frustrated with the winter. When storms happen, be ready, go through them. Hold to the dreams and visions.

Bob Dylan turned Ecclesiastes chapter 3 into a song made popular by the Byrds: "To everything turn, turn, turn—there is a season, turn, turn, turn. And a time for every purpose under heaven."[2] It resonates with listeners and is a classic because seasons are in our original, God-given DNA. Seasons change. Seeds are planted, watered, cultivated, and harvested in different seasons.

"Seedtime and harvest" is one the most important principles of the Bible. It's one of the most important principles of the world we live in.

The apostle Paul wrote, "God will not be mocked, whatever is sowed will be reaped."[3] The seeds you plant today determine the harvest you have tomorrow. Plant good seed—reap a good harvest. Plant bad seed—well, you get it—bad harvest.

When you are planting good seeds in your life, the enemy wants to kill them. It seems like guys who are planting bad seeds don't have as many obstacles. I think that's true. Might have something to do with a world that celebrates bad seeds.

Don't be that guy. Plant good seed, stay in touch with your season.

Be faithful in your season. Thrive.

21
ALLIES

Faithful men become strong men. I've said hundreds of times, "Strong men make strong families and strong families make strong churches." Jesus told his men, *"I will build my church, and all the powers of hell will not conquer it."*[1] That's the goal. When we build strong men and strong families, we build strong churches. That's God's plan to bring healing and wholeness to the entire world.

Paul wrote to his protégé, "Timothy, find faithful men, who will be *able....*"[2] The faithful man is empowered by the Spirit of God to be *able*. He is *able* to do things he couldn't do on his own.

Jesus never asked fully ready men to follow Him. Until Jesus shows up, no one is ready.

Jesus just says, "Follow Me." As we follow Jesus, He mentors us, builds us, fashions us into His image. He makes us "ready."

Jesus' followers never become *perfect* men. We become *faithful* men. As we are faithful to follow Him, He builds our lives. It's a process. Just because we follow Him doesn't make us disciples. As we grow in faith and faithfulness and focus, we become disciples.

A swirl of light snow chilled the January air and left a layer of ice on the ground. People in Starbucks were ordering hot coffee and cider while checking their phones to see if the temperature would rise. They needed warm air to keep from slipping and sliding into each other, as often happens on North Texas roads in ice storms. I was hoping I could get to the hospital but wasn't sure, so I texted.

JESUS NEVER ASKED FULLY READY MEN TO FOLLOW HIM. UNTIL JESUS SHOWS UP, NO ONE IS READY.

Steve and I were friends. Brothers. I had his back, and he had mine. He was struggling through brain cancer. I visited him as often as I was in town, and we texted more often. That morning I texted him, "Steve, I'm praying for you every day. It's a new year, a year of deliverance. I believe it. I'm with you. PC."

"Thanks," he wrote back. "Love you," I texted back. Pause. Then his next text came in. "Every day?" I wrote back, "Yes, every day." Pause. Then he wrote, "Dude, no offense, but should I be looking for another intercessor who could get more tangible results?"

What a funny, wonderful, godly man. I sure miss him. I read those texts at his memorial service. He was someone I could hang with. Someone who showed up for me. A guy I didn't need to impress, and I didn't need him to impress me. An ally whom I could talk to at my toughest moments. And I was there for his.

Paul talked about this in his second letter to Timothy. Timothy had been raised by his mom and grandmother, and now he needed a strong man. Paul saw greatness in him. Paul mentored him. Then Paul put him in charge of a huge church and wrote out instructions for him.

"And the things that you have heard from me among many witnesses, commit these to faithful men who will be able to teach others also," Paul

wrote.[3] The verse is multi-generational. Paul is talking about himself, and Tim, and the men Tim was mentoring, and finally, the men those men would mentor. Four generations. The main qualification for all these men is one word: faithful.

Faithfulness is the foundation of godly character. Most of us look up to men with great ability or awesome talent—someone who lights up a room when he walks in. Too many men work on their talent and not on their character. Many get successful based on talent and then crash and burn. We often see this with sports stars, leaders in industry, politics, and the pulpit. Their talent takes them to a place that their character can't sustain.

One of the most amazing men who ever lived was Abraham. He was faithful to follow God, even when he didn't know where God was leading. Abraham is called the "Father of the Faith." In the book of James, he explained the secret ingredient of Abraham's life. It's this: he was called the "*friend of God.*"[4]

Abraham had an encounter with God. God promised that if Abraham would faithfully follow him, God would make him the father of a great nation.[5] At that point, Abraham was a seventy-five-year-old childless man with no heir. But now, he had a promise. Finally, something to hold on to.

Abraham was not a perfect man. He followed God, but he made some poor decisions. One big mistake, a masterful *oops*. Although the promised heir, a son called Isaac, was supposed to come through his wife Sarah, they got impatient. Sarah wasn't getting pregnant. So she offered him her maid Hagar—he didn't refuse. He could have said, "Sorry Sarah, you know I'm trusting God—sleep with your maid? No way." That didn't happen. Sarah was frustrated. He was impatient. Impatience can kill your promise.

Abraham had a promise, but he stepped out on his own and had a son by a young maid named Hagar. That boy was called Ishmael. Wrong guy. When Sarah finally had Isaac, Ishmael became a sworn enemy of Isaac. The son of impatience desired to kill the son of promise. After Sarah died, Abraham married Keturah and had six more sons. The offspring of those sons also became enemies of Isaac. Hundreds of years later, we often still see the children of Isaac attacked by the children of his half-brothers. Abraham's impatience echoes across the centuries.

WHATEVER WE CREATE OUTSIDE THE PROMISE WILL ALWAYS TRY TO KILL THE PROMISE.

Isaac was the promise. But Abraham made decisions outside the promise. Whatever Abraham did outside his instructions from God ended up negative. Everything Abraham did outside the promise tried to kill the promise. Whatever we create outside the promise will always try to kill the promise.

Abraham made some bad decisions, *but* he followed God. He was tested repeatedly, *but* he persevered. Abraham finished his life strong. His real secret through it all was simply this: he was a friend of God's.

A friend is faithful.

"As iron sharpens iron, so a friend sharpens a friend."[6]

"A friend loves at all times, and a brother is born for a time of adversity."[7]

A friend is someone who talks good about you behind your back…

A friend is life's shock absorber…

A friend brightens the room when he enters. (Others may brighten it when they leave.)

A brother is not necessarily a friend, but a friend is always a brother.

Isaac's own brothers weren't his friends. My friend Rod Anderson taught me what the expression "blood is thicker than water" really means. In almost every culture around the world, blood is a sign of covenant—usually blood from fingers, hands, or animals. The saying "blood is thicker than water" means two men in blood covenant are closer, more committed to each other, than two men who may have been born from the same birth water. It's about being in covenant. Friends. Allies.

The blood that Jesus shed on the cross was a sign and signature of covenant. That's why we can be assured Jesus is a *"friend who sticks closer than a brother."*[8]

———————

There's a great story about Jesus and one of His best friends, Lazarus. Lazarus was at home in Bethany, sick and about to die. Lazarus's sisters sent word to a nearby town for Jesus to come heal him, "and hurry!"

John, who wrote the story, never says that Lazarus was worried. It seems he trusted his friend. But those around Lazarus didn't share his faith—they were freaking.

Jesus and Lazarus had been friends for some time, but now it seemed their friendship was being tested. Instead of rushing to His friend, Jesus stayed in a nearby town teaching. Then He got word that Lazarus was dead. His friend was gone, but—it seems crazy—Jesus still waited for a couple *more* days.

Jesus had a plan, a strategy. It was wisdom beyond earthly wisdom, and it was happening in real time. Four days after His friend's death, Jesus arrives in Bethany to a frosty reception. The sisters are upset. Jesus endures the blame, then tells Lazarus's sisters and the other mourners who have gathered, "Relax, I've got this." Or words to that effect.

Jesus walks over to the tomb that holds the body of Lazarus, wrapped and laid out inside. He commands the local men to roll away the stone covering the mouth of the tomb. Martha resists. In King James English, Martha says, *"Lord, by this time he stinketh!"*[9] The men roll the stone away and Jesus shouts out His friend's name. "LAZARUS!" He yells, "COME OUT!"[10]

Boom. Lazarus comes out. People start yelling and crying. It's pandemonium. The place is stunned and word spreads, fast. For months after this, Lazarus tells his story to hundreds of people. There's always someone around wanting to hear it, wanting to see him, to shake hands with the guy who died. The story gets so big that the religious leaders are fearful. People who have seen Lazarus are starting to follow Christ. So, when the religious leaders plot to kill Jesus, they decide they need to kill Lazarus as well.

Jesus and Lazarus were friends. They were in it together. Because of Lazarus's story, God was able to move His divine plan forward for Jesus to be betrayed and killed, as a sacrifice for the sins of all humanity. What looked like a total failure was a massive win.

A true friend is your brother.

When we are in covenant with God through Christ, we're able to be men of our word. We're able to be men who are there for our brothers. We're covenant men.

Greater love has no one than this, than to lay down one's life for his friends.

> You are My friends if you do whatever I command you. No longer do I call you servants, for a servant does not know what his master is doing; but I have called you friends, for all things that I heard from My Father I have made known to you.
>
> You did not choose Me, but I chose you and appointed you that you should go and bear fruit, and that your fruit should remain, that whatever you ask the Father in My name He may give you.
>
> These things I command you, that you love one another.[11]

You gain friends by being a friend.[12] Go be a friend to someone. Allies.

22

COURAGE

I was on my way home from Turkey—just wrapping up an intense ten-day trip, talking to men as I always do wherever they are—Oklahoma, Belize, Germany, Jakarta, Kampala. Sitting in La Guardia, I looked forward to this last flight to the DFW airport. In just a few hours, I'd be home. I was tired but also energized by the results we were seeing. God transforming the hearts of men.

In 1977, my father, Ed Cole, was pastoring a local church in Costa Mesa, California. He flew up to speak at a men's camp in Oregon and at that meeting God placed in his heart the dream to launch a ministry that would specialize in mentoring and discipling men.

What he had discovered in years of pastoring was that most pastors were taught how to preach sermons, not how to disciple men. So most men were taught to listen to sermons, not to study the Word of God. That philosophy produced a generation of men that let their pastors do the heavy lifting of the ministry while they watched and paid his salary. The men felt absolved from responsibility because, hey, they paid the preacher to reach the city, take care of their kids, and make sure it all came out right. Wrong.

The results of that kind of thinking resulted in churches full of wussy, weak, flaccid, narrow-thinking men, and churches with no influence in the real life of the community. Church became where a man went to get his "You're An Okay Guy" stamp and then go live in whatever way he thought best the rest of the week.

My dad began driving a van across the country telling men it was time to stand up and be real men. To be a real man was to be like Jesus, because manhood and Christlikeness are synonymous. He wrote a book, *Maximized Manhood*, that went around the world. He launched a new generation of ministry to men. His ministry changed the world.

Now, more than a decade after his passing, Judi and I, our family, and my sisters and their families are picking up the same fight. My family and I today live that legacy. Dad's courage has outlived him.

Courage. The leaders gathered in Turkey had moved me deeply. Most of them were in underground churches throughout difficult areas in the Middle East. Others were in visible churches but still dealt with tremendous persecution. Though from many countries, their joint times of worship soared. I turned on my recorder to capture it. The stories I heard that week were hard to fathom, humbling. To men in the West, these are the unknown heroes of faith.

One man told me his story. I'll call him Mert, which is Turkish for "brave and manly"—because that's what he is. He had found Jesus as his Savior in his home country (not Turkey) in an interesting way.

As a young man, Mert had a longing in his heart for a personal relationship with God. He had been taught that his religion was the true faith, but it left him empty. There was no relationship, just a series of laws and regulations you adhered to or you would be killed. He'd heard the word "Christian" and was told that that religion was different.

One day a tourist was taking a photo on the public square in Mert's city and Mert, hurrying through, literally bumped into him. The tourist was very kind about the accident—too kind. Mert felt something about the tourist was different. Although such words were not spoken aloud in his country, he blurted in broken English, "Are you a Christian?"

The tourist replied, "Yes."

Mert lowered his voice and asked, "Can you tell me about Jesus?" For about ten minutes, the tourist told Mert the story of Christ.

Mert wanted more. He found a Bible at an underground market. "You can buy anything in the underground," he told me with a smile.

He devoured the Bible. It made sense to him. Three years later, he moved to northern Turkey to study in college. There, he opened a church with a legal license—the only Christian church in a city of two million people. Mert rented an empty store in a small building and opened the church. The local Islamic leaders were so incensed they organized protests. Day after day, they didn't picket, they just came out and stood. Their presence kept most people from attending.

Mert and three of his friends prayed daily inside the little storefront church. Then the local TV station broadcast a story about the protests. Mert was certain the news story would get them shut down for good. He prayed hard through the night.

The day after the broadcast, a chauffeur pulled a large car up to the line of the protesters. A man sprang from the backseat wearing an expensive dark suit and sunglasses. He walked up to the line and told the protestors to move. They did. He walked through the front door and found Mert inside, praying.

The man said, "Are you the teacher that they are all mad about?"

"Yes."

"I saw the story," he said. "I am not a Christian but I believe they are wrong to protest what is legal to do. We are a country that must love all people. So, here is some money for you to buy this little building. And, I will send money over to you every month for a year to get you started. May you have the blessings of your God."

He turned around to leave, then looked over his shoulder at Mert and said offhandedly, "You will not have any more protestors."

The man left. The protestors left.

It took courage for Mert to withstand the onslaught of protestors and TV broadcasts. He stood strong and God produced a miracle. When I met Mert, more than one hundred people had met Jesus Christ at his little fully-paid-for church building.

This was just one of the stories I had heard as I met with these brave leaders. I boarded my flight with a full heart.

The next afternoon, I got my wife Judi and played the recording I made of those church leaders singing. We both cried. Just recalling that wonderful, liberating sound still touches my heart as I write today, three years later. Here's why: I turned to the leader next to me during the singing. I raised my voice and said, "They're singing so *loud*." He said, "Yes, because in their home countries, they cannot sing out loud at all."

The singing we were listening to was the sound of *courage*.

———————

Courage is the result of embraced destiny.

In the life of Nehemiah, one thing stands out—this man had courage. He had an inner resolve that would not give up in the face of adversity. He would rather have died than give up his dream. His dream became his identity. The embracing of that identity filled him with courage.

Today, when a man fully commits his life to Jesus Christ, he receives a new heart, a fresh beginning, and something very important. When he really commits, he receives courage.

Courage is staying in the game when others quit. Courage is staying in your marriage when others tell you it's OK to leave. Courage is launching a church in the toughest part of town. Courage is facing critics and keeping your cool. Courage is not turning back in the face of a fight.

Courage is unseen—but if a man has courage, you *will* see results.

Courage is having the guts to stand for your convictions.

Courage doesn't just happen. It's not something a man is born with. Remember, we are born risk averse. We are born to avoid confrontation. In the military, what has to be trained out of a warrior is the physical urge to run from danger...to take flight.

COURAGE DOESN'T JUST HAPPEN. COURAGE IS BUILT.

Courage is built. The Word of God gives a man courage. Knowing his identity gives a man courage. Having values that are worth fighting for gives a man courage. Knowing right from wrong and then committing to right gives a man courage.

Jesus said it like this to the men around him:

> *"The Father is with me. I've told you all this so that **trusting me, you will be unshakable** and assured, deeply at peace. In this godless world you will continue to experience difficulties. But take heart! I've conquered the world."*[1]

Hundreds of years earlier, God told Joshua as they faced huge obstacles, "Take courage!" When you trust that God has your back, that's the start of spiritual courage.

In the valleys of northern Iraq, the Islamic State is slaughtering Christians—killing boys and girls, moms, dads, and entire families. We know from news reports that many are even buried alive. We see pictures of the refugee camps of our Christian brothers and sisters. We see pictures of people running for their lives—thrust into the desert, on the verge of starvation and within miles of the evil national armies. Tragic. Horrible.

Christian activist and author Johnnie Moore explains that these Christians have been told, "If we find out you are a Christian, you and your family will die an unspeakable death. Convert to Islam or die."

Yet, the response of these Christians is never to renounce Christ, but to encourage each other that "it will only hurt for a minute."

In photos of the refugee camps, there is one very noteworthy item visible over the sea of tents and people. In response to the threats of the terrorists, prominent on each tent is a cross. Not only that, but every tent has a light that shines on the cross. In the deepening sky of twilight those crosses stand out like beacons of hope. And they shine as courageous statement to the enemy. They say, "If you come here, we want you to know, just so there is no mistake, we are Christians. And you can kill us, but we will not give up our faith!"

Courage.

23

STANDARD

Nehemiah and the workers built the walls of Jerusalem in fifty-two days, leaving until the end some of the ramparts, palisades, towers, and the massive piers and guardrooms for the gates. When Nehemiah first surveyed the city, he couldn't even get his horse through some of the gates because of rubble. Now, as he appointed gatekeepers, the city was secure.

Raising the walls restored national pride. Over the next few months over 50,000 people made their way back to Jerusalem. It was an ancient, "If you build it, they will come."[1]

Not everyone was thrilled. The regional kings were furious. Nehemiah had done nothing to antagonize them, had not sent threats flying back after their threats came. He had simply followed what God directed him to do, what his king provided for him to do—and it made people mad. Raising the walls raised a standard of who God is. It represented His identity as a God of restoration and renewal. It showed that His people, unified in vision, could accomplish anything.

Today, God rebuilds people. The church, meaning all of us as Christ-followers collectively, raise the identity of God as righteous, holy, and loving. As we raise a standard of righteousness, the kings of the earth—the thought-makers of secular culture—get mad. They become "Christophobic"—meaning, they're antagonistic to Christianity without any basis other than their personal prejudice.

The Bible says that when we raise a standard, people are judged by their comparison to the standard. As Christians, we are not to judge people but to raise a standard. Just like Nehemiah, when we raise the standard, we will be threatened and the world will be upset.

After Nehemiah completed construction, his next priority was to keep the people safe and to honor God. He stationed men with weapons in the gates to protect the new inhabitants, and gave the Jewish citizens special registration cards. Then he commissioned the priests to get ready for a time of worship and celebration. Swords and worship music....

I've heard many people who speak of Jesus as a morally strong but highly sensitive, almost delicate Man. They mistake graciousness for weakness. Never mistake kindness on the outside for softness on the inside.

It was the strength of Jesus on the inside that allowed Him to be gracious on the outside. A man who is weak on the inside always tries to prove his strength on the outside. He's a dictator with his family, demanding of his employees, and proud of his accomplishments, whether that's today's business or from years past in high school sports—it always comes up.

A man who is strong in his heart doesn't have to prove it. He just is.

One of our dear friends who passed away at a young age was the Hall of Fame football player Reggie White. I remember Reggie at our home one evening, playing with our boys when they were young. They were climbing all over him, wrestling and playing hard like he was just another friend. They had fun. He was loving, gentle, and full of joy. A few days later, I watched him reach out and take a huge, powerful player on the Cowboys football team, sling him out of the way and sack quarterback Troy Aikman, all in a matter of seconds. He was big, fast, and didn't have to prove it. He knew who he was.

THE STRENGTH OF A MAN IS IN HIS HEART.

The strength of a man is in his heart. He doesn't have to prove it. It will show.

One of the men who met Nehemiah in Jerusalem was another great man named Ezra. He was a righteous man, a prophet, and a priest. Ezra took out the old scrolls of Scripture that had been stored in the broken temple.

A few months later, the people gathered inside the walls of the city. By then, houses and businesses were being rebuilt, the roads cleared of debris. A city square was opened for the people to gather.

They read the Holy Scriptures, prayed, and rejoiced. They began an eight-day festival of worship, prayer, and feasting that is still celebrated today in Israel.

Nehemiah was the governor and things were going well. Just one big issue. He had promised King Artaxerxes that he would return to Persia when the walls were finished. He'd been gone for some time now. Things were good. But he knew he had to go back. The man now enjoying the rewards of rebuilding the city, leading several thousand people, would go back to his job as a bartender. It was his job, but it no longer defined him.

Nehemiah, the slave and bartender—the last man anyone would have expected—had rebuilt Jerusalem to lead a nation back from near extinction. He succeeded. It was unexpected.

I'm sure Nehemiah thought about this. Did he really want to go back to being a bartender and slave? But he'd given his word. He was a man of integrity. Your integrity will prove your maturity.

A mature man does the right thing. A mature man is not swayed by the emotions of the moment. This is still one of the greatest issues facing our world. Immature men act like children. Men can stay immature for years…or for a lifetime.

God wants men to be mature. To be strong, decisive, and consistent. Maturity comes from accepting responsibility for your actions. Maturity is the discipline to make the right decision even when the emotions or context of the moment would tempt us to do the wrong thing.

Remember, temptation to sin is not sin. It's what we do with the temptation that causes us to sin.

Immaturity compromises. Nehemiah went back to Persia and worked for the king for a few years. The great leader was once again a slave. But he was not defined by the work he did. His identity was settled long before.

God never puts your destiny in the hands of your enemy!

Nehemiah was a slave, but a short time later, the king set him free to return once again to Jerusalem. This time, Nehemiah marched into Jerusalem a free man.

Yet when Nehemiah returned, he rode into a mess. It wasn't because people had started living deeply immoral lives. It was because of one small compromise at a time. They had become comfortable in yesterday's victories. Looking back will never take you forward. Like the walls that decayed, one stone at a time—a small compromise, a brief look the other way, the small distraction. Without anything seeming to be a big deal, the whole city had fallen apart.

A man following Christ does not have the option to compromise with sin.

Evil is simply accepting what is contrary to the Word of God— accepting what is wrong and saying it's OK. God says that He hates people who say evil is good and good is evil.[2]

Nehemiah recorded that when he returned to Jerusalem, he actually beat up some guys who simply would not accept correction. I don't recommend this. But it illustrates Nehemiah's intolerance for what was evil. He got his point across.

There is a powerful old Andean parable of a man hiking through snow and ice high in the mountains. On the side of the trail, he found a poisonous snake, a viper, freezing to death. The snake said, "Please help me," so the hiker took pity and put the viper inside his jacket. The snake and the hiker journeyed back down the mountain. At the bottom, in the warmth of the day, the hiker took the snake out of his jacket and gently put it on the ground. That's when the snake fatally bit him. The hiker was shocked, his life ebbing away. He said to the snake, "I took care of you. I rescued you and saved your life. Why did you kill me?" The snake said, "You fool. You knew I was a viper when you picked me up."

Too many men fall into compromise, just a little here, little there, thinking they can step back from the edge just before they are ruined. Too many men pick up poisonous snakes and think they can evade the bite. Many are dying today because of it. Don't be that fool—don't grasp death and hold it to your chest.

***

A politician and socialite who could out-sing his companions, out-argue his peers, provide wit and humor to every conversation, and gamble like a sailor, had a profound experience with Christ in the privacy of his own contemplation. The popular William Wilberforce became a Member of Parliament when he was just twenty-one years old. At age twenty-six, he and a traveling companion started reading Christian literature. A study of Scripture led William to commit his life to Christ and to Christian work.

At first, William was going to leave politics, thinking his Christianity and a political career could not mix. But a close friend who had become Prime Minister convinced him to stay. A year later, William found out why. God had a mission for him, an assignment for him to accomplish, and it became his dream.

William became incensed by the mortality rate among slaves and the deplorable conditions in which slaves lived. He became one of the most outspoken proponents of the abolitionist movement. Time after time, proposals were made to stem the tide of slavery, to guarantee freedoms, or to remedy slaves' living conditions. Time after time, the government outmaneuvered William and his friends.

Frail from birth, William's health steadily declined, as did his fortune, and even his popularity. When he was seventy-four years old, he made his last speech, and the government introduced the final "Bill for the Abolition of Slavery." This time it passed, and William was honored by his peers. Three months later, William died.

Wilberforce never saw the full effects of his efforts. But he had already seen it in his dreams, his vision—and he would not be distracted.

Raising a standard may cost you. It may not make you popular—but it will make you effective.

24

FAVOR

He roars up in his 4x4 truck—jacked up, big wheels and tires, a Rhino roll bar and a thumping Rockford Fosgate sound system that costs more than the computer I'm typing on right now. I watch as Jesse slams to a stop at Redefined, a coffee shop where we're going to have a talk about his future that he doesn't even know is coming. I've counseled, been a friend, Judi and I have had him in our home, and in my heart I feel that today is the day. I have to confront him with hard truth.

Jesse walks in with his backpack just as I leave the counter with a flat white for me, an Americano for him. We sit alone outside and get right into it. But Jesse surprises me. He says, "Hey, I need to make a change." That's an understatement. I lean in and listen. He opens his backpack and pulls out two red For Sale signs. "I'm putting the truck up for sale."

I lean back, laughing, "You're kidding me!"

"No, not kidding," he says, as he puts them back. "You know, I love it. But it's holding me back. My whole identity is wrapped up in that truck. Man, my identity has to be in more than what I drive!"

"Wisdom!" I hit his shoulder then get serious. "Jesse, I wanted to tell you today that it really is time. You really need to pray that prayer."

"Nehemiah's prayer," he says. He had seen it coming. Came prepared.

"Yeah, the prayer I've been telling you about."

The prayer isn't long. But it's one of the most powerful prayers in the Bible. That prayer launched the most unexpected man in the world to rebuild the city of Jerusalem. Nehemiah rebuilt the walls that had been built a more than 500 years before by King David. He became the man who rebuilt the gates of a Holy City that 450 years later Jesus would walk through.

Jesse and I pray Nehemiah's prayer.[1] Our paraphrase goes like this:

Dear God, Lord of heaven and earth, my Father in heaven who keeps His covenant of unfailing love toward those who love Him and obey His commands, thank You for listening to my prayer!

I thank You for Your son Jesus, and for the forgiveness I have because of Him. I confess from my heart that I have sinned against You and Your Word. I live in a sinful world. Thank You for forgiving me. I pray for forgiveness for my nation and my culture.

You said if we would ask You to forgive us that You would. That You would clean my heart and my life and make me a new creation. You promised Nehemiah that You would restore his nation if people were faithful to You. And You did. You have always kept Your word. You promised never to leave me. That You would give me Your presence, the Holy Spirit, to guide me, to strengthen me, restore me, and help me to become everything You designed me to be. I commit my life again today, totally and fully to You.

Father God, You have never stopped loving me, and Your strong hand has rescued me. My life belongs to You.

Now, I ask dear Father, for great success. I ask for favor with people and leaders. I ask that You would always be with me, even as You promised. I ask You to keep my heart safe and free from sin. To guide me into the purpose You created me for. I ask for the redemption of all mankind and for the salvation of my entire family and all my friends. In the name of Jesus, Amen.

It's a spectacular morning. The warmth of the moment is mirrored by the Texas sun climbing over the buildings to the east. We walk to our cars. In the movies, it would have been a longer moment. But we're guys, and we don't live in the movies. So we slap a handshake, then a quick embrace. I tell him I'll pray for him every day. As he pulls out, he yells through the passenger window, "Hey man, thanks!"

Judi and I talk about Jesse late that night. It is hard for either of us to believe he's the same guy. A changed life is all about God.

As men, we find our identity when we lose our identity in Christ. First you accept responsibility for your mistakes, then you accept God's forgiveness, then in His strength, you forgive yourself. We tend to make it complex, but it's pretty straightforward.

As theologian Alexander MacLaren wrote, "No man will do worthy work at rebuilding the walls who has not first wept over the ruins."[2]

The next day I hit the airport headed out of town. Another city. Another opportunity. As I sit down in the plane, I get a text....

"Truck already sold. It's favor, bro. Doing the stuff! Jesse."

I'm sure people look at me and wonder why I'm sitting on the plane all alone with a big goofy smile. It was unexpected.

Nehemiah. A bartender, a slave—just a guy. Unexpected people....

EPILOGUE

This book is more than the collected words…it's about sounds, colors, a call, a cause—a trumpet blowing in the distance, and coming this direction. It's about urgency and work and effort and sweat and Jesus. It's about strong coffee and strong friendships and strong men and strong churches and guys who fall down but get back up.

It's about men who dream and then put a date on the dream. It's about grown-up men who don't back down when they are smacked in the face or misunderstood or rejected or the room's too hot or too cold or the meeting goes too long. It's not about convenience and comfort. It's about character, courage, conviction, and the cross.

They may not be pretty words—but I pray they're words that will paint brilliant and powerful pictures in your heart, that will stir you to a new level of life. I've been deeply challenged writing this. We all have so many imperfections. I listen so easily to other voices, so easily lean into wanting to be liked rather than speaking hard truth…but I'm not going to let go of the dream. I'm underlining my own book… doing the work.

Most of the stories on these pages were written about men I know well. I changed names and often occupations to allow them space to continue writing their own stories. But all of them, as well as the coffee, are as real as the stones of Jerusalem. I cried over a lot of their stories as I wrote. Real guys with real issues. Real victories, real defeats. All I did, all any friend can do, is help create a way of access to the Father. Only God can change a man's heart. The power of the Holy Spirit must be embraced. It's not about explanation or information, it's always about revelation. It's always about Jesus.

Your life is about the story you tell yourself about yourself. Your identity. That internal compass that directs your decisions, that guides your life. You've got to work—hard—to defeat the negativity of our world, and the messages we so easily succumb to. Do the work to tune in to the voice that tells you that you're valuable, that you have courage, that you can make it, that you don't have to give in to lust or jealousy or the compromise of the moment. That's His voice—the defining voice of our Father.

My prayer is that you'll do the work, find a fresh vision, and be willing to pray Nehemiah's prayer for yourself:

> Dear God, Lord of heaven and earth, my Father in heaven who keeps His covenant of unfailing love toward those who love Him and obey His commands, thank You for listening to my prayer!
>
> I thank You for Your son Jesus, and for the forgiveness I have because of Him. I confess from my heart that I have sinned against You and Your Word. I live in a sinful world. Thank You for forgiving me. I pray for forgiveness for my nation and my culture.
>
> You said if we would ask You to forgive us that You would. That You would clean my heart and my life and make me a new creation. You promised Nehemiah that You would restore his nation if people were faithful to You. And You did. You have always kept Your word. You promised never to leave me. That You would give me Your presence, the Holy Spirit, to guide me, to strengthen me, restore me, and help me to become everything You designed me to be. I commit my life again today, totally and fully to You.

Father God, You have never stopped loving me, and Your strong hand has rescued me. My life belongs to You.

Now, I ask dear Father, for great success. I ask for favor with people and leaders. I ask that You would always be with me, even as You promised. I ask You to keep my heart safe and free from sin. To guide me into the purpose You created me for. I ask for the redemption of all mankind and for the salvation of my entire family and all my friends. In the name of Jesus, Amen.

Live strong—love well—laugh loud—hug often—grow flowers and grow warriors. Too many men live in the gray zone. God doesn't live in the shadows—He lives in the bright light of freedom.

This isn't the end of a book. This is the start of you becoming what you've always wanted to become, doing what you've always wanted to do. Go strong after your dream. I believe in you. God believes in you. You are—*the unexpected man.*

ENDNOTES

Chapter 1
1. Psalm 122:6.
2. Don Henly and Glenn Frey, "Desperado" (Atlantic Records, 1973).
3. Proverbs 4:23 MSG.

Chapter 2
1. Jeremiah 29:11, author's paraphrase.
2. Colossians 3:23; see also Ecclesiastes 9:10.
3. AMP.
4. NKJV.

Chapter 3
1. Nehemiah 1:5–7 NLT.
2. Nehemiah 1:8–9.
3. Nehemiah 1:10–11 NIV.
4. James 4:2–3, author's paraphrase.
5. Ephesians 1:5–6, author's paraphrase.
6. Ephesians 1:6 KJV.
7. See Luke 1:28 NIV and KJV.
8. Judges 6:12.
9. See Genesis 37:3.
10. Exodus 3:12; see Genesis 12:1–3.
11. Matthew 28:20 MSG.

Chapter 4
1. Nick Vujicic, *Life Without Limits* (New York: Crown Publishing Group, 2012), 37.
2. Theodore Roosevelt, "The Strenuous Life," *The Strenuous Life: Essays and Addresses* (New York: The Century Co., 1900, published online February 1998 by bartleby.com).
3. James 2:26 NKJV.
4. Hebrews 10:36, author's paraphrase.
5. General George Patton, GeneralPatton.com, http://www.generalpatton.com/quotes/ (accessed 10/3/16).
6. Widely attributed to Calvin Coolidge, this quotation first appeared in a 1930s pamphlet printed by New York Life Insurance Co.

Chapter 5
1. Nehemiah 2:2, author's paraphrase.
2. Nehemiah 2:3–5, author's paraphrase.

Chapter 6
1. John 3:16 NKJV.
2. See 2 Kings 4:1–7.
3. Isaiah 32:7–8 NLT.
4. Isaiah 32:8 NLT

Chapter 7
1. See James 2:17.

Chapter 8

1. Psalm 119:11, author's paraphrase.
2. Proverbs 4:23, author's paraphrase.
3. Matthew 22:36–40, author's paraphrase.
4. Ross Perot, "Ross Perot Quotes," Brainyquote.com, http://www.brainyquote.com/quotes/quotes/r/rossperot101658.html (accessed 10/3/16).

Chapter 9

1. John 20:23, author's paraphrase.

Chapter 10

1. Hebrews 13:5 AMPC.

Chapter 11

1. Genesis 3:1.
2. 2 Corinthians 5:17, author's paraphrase.

Chapter 12

1. 1 Corinthians 9:24–27 NLT-1996.
2. Sam Charles Sarkesian, ed., *Revolutionary Guerilla Warfare* (Piscataway, NJ: Transaction Publishers, 2010), 167.
3. Hosea 7:16 TLB.

Chapter 13

1. 2 Timothy 1:7, author's paraphrase.
2. See Psalm 23.
3. See Mark 5:36; Matthew 14:27; 6:34; John 14:27; Isaiah 46:4; Matthew 25:21.
4. Romans 5:3–5 NLT.

Chapter 14

1. John Steinbeck, "Private letter to Elizabeth Otis," *Steinbeck: A Life in Letters*, MondayMorningMemo.com, http://www.mondaymorningmemo.com/shinyeasythings-steinbeck/ (accessed 2/15/17).
2. See Luke 16:11.

Chapter 15

1. Matthew 4:4 NLT.
2. Psalm 119:11 NLT.
3. See Matthew 4:10.
4. NLT.
5. 1 John 1:9 NLT.

Chapter 16

1. Geoff Gorsuch, *Brothers!* (Colorado Springs, CO: NavPress 1994), 34.
2. Proverbs 8:23.
3. Proverbs 4:7 KJV.
4. James 3:14–15.
5. 2 Corinthians 1:12.
6. See Matthew 18:18–19.
7. Isaiah 61:3, author's paraphrase.

Chapter 17

1. Romans 12:2, author's paraphrase.
2. Nehemiah 4:17, author's paraphrase.
3. See Nehemiah 2:6.
4. Nehemiah 4:14 NLT.
5. Nehemiah 4:20 NLT.

Chapter 18

1. Nehemiah 6:11, author's paraphrase.

Chapter 19

1. John 16:33 NLT.
2. Romans 12:12 NLT.
3. James 1:2–4 NLT.
4. See Zechariah 4:6.
5. See 1 Samuel 16–17.
6. See Romans 8:37.
7. Luke 4:18–19 NLT.

Chapter 20

1. Luke 4:18–19 NLT.
2. Pete Seeger, "Turn! Turn! Turn!" (Columbia, 1965).
3. Galatians 6:7, author's paraphrase.

Chapter 21

1. Matthew 16:18 NLT.
2. 2 Timothy 2:2, author's paraphrase.
3. 2 Timothy 2:2 NKJV.
4. James 2:23 NLT.
5. Genesis 15.
6. Proverbs 27:17 NLT.
7. Proverbs 17:17.
8. Proverbs 18:24 NKJV.
9. John 11:39 KJV.
10. See John 11:38–44.
11. John 15:14–17 NKJV.
12. See Proverbs 18:24 KJV.

Chapter 22

1. John 16:32–33 MSG.

Chapter 23

1. Phil Alden Robinson, *Field of Dreams*, adapted from W. P. Kinsella's novel, *Shoeless Joe* (Universal Pictures, 1989).
2. See Isaiah 5:20.

Chapter 24

1. Nehemiah 1, author's paraphrase.
2. *MacLaren's Expositions*, Nehemiah 1:1–11, Biblehub.com, http://biblehub.com/commentaries/nehemiah/1-1.htm (accessed 8/28/15).

ABOUT CHRISTIAN MEN'S NETWORK

For forty years, the ministry of Christian Men's Network has worked to win men to Christ. Cofounded by Edwin Louis Cole and his family, the ministry today is vibrant in over 100 nations and in 80 languages. CMN has created powerful tools to build successful men for a highly motivated church. Embraced by Christian leaders worldwide, it is the most widely-used, time-proven men's discipleship model in the world. Nearly two million men have become "maximized" in their manhood through this simple yet effective outreach to men.

To host a men's event in your area or at your church, to launch MAJORING IN MEN® training at your church, or to receive additional information about ministry to men, contact Christian Men's Network.

ChristianMensNetwork.com

P. O. Box 3
Grapevine, TX 76099
817-437-4888

ABOUT THE AUTHOR

Paul Louis Cole, DTh, president of Christian Men's Network, is a communicator, church planter, pastor, author, and one of the world's leading experts on men's issues. Paul is an award-winning media writer/producer/director, but his passion is in carrying the message of Christlike manhood globally. The son of Edwin Louis Cole, he has continued the work of the Christian Men's Network, helping pastors build strong men, strong families, and strong churches in over 100 nations. Paul's mission is to rescue men, defeat fatherlessness, and end child abuse by providing leadership tools and strategies to bring a clear and defining word to men.

Paul and his wife of forty-plus years, Judi, reside in Grapevine, Texas. They have three children and five grandchildren.